50 Chocolate Dessert Recipes for Home

By: Kelly Johnson

Table of Contents

- Chocolate Lava Cake
- Chocolate Mousse
- Chocolate Fondue
- Chocolate Truffles
- Chocolate Soufflé
- Chocolate Cheesecake
- Chocolate Brownies
- Chocolate Tiramisu
- Chocolate Silk Pie
- Chocolate Covered Strawberries
- Chocolate Banana Bread
- Chocolate Chip Cookies
- Chocolate Pudding
- Chocolate Eclairs
- Chocolate Creme Brulee
- Chocolate Coconut Macaroons
- Chocolate Raspberry Tart
- Chocolate Peanut Butter Cups
- Chocolate Cherry Trifle
- Chocolate Caramel Slice
- Chocolate Hazelnut Tart
- Chocolate Peppermint Bark
- Chocolate Bread Pudding
- Chocolate Marshmallow Bars
- Chocolate Orange Cake
- Chocolate Almond Biscotti
- Chocolate Cream Pie
- Chocolate Toffee Crunch
- Chocolate Dipped Pretzels
- Chocolate Rice Krispie Treats
- Chocolate Strawberry Shortcake
- Chocolate Pistachio Cake
- Chocolate Cinnamon Rolls
- Chocolate Macadamia Nut Cookies
- Chocolate Peanut Butter Brownies

- Chocolate Espresso Cake
- Chocolate Mint Ice Cream
- Chocolate Coconut Pudding
- Chocolate Walnut Fudge
- Chocolate Caramel Macarons
- Chocolate Bourbon Pecan Pie
- Chocolate Cherry Clafoutis
- Chocolate Custard Tart
- Chocolate Hazelnut Biscotti
- Chocolate Raspberry Cheesecake
- Chocolate Pecan Pie Bars
- Chocolate Toffee Trifle
- Chocolate Gingerbread Cake
- Chocolate Caramel Cheesecake
- Chocolate Blueberry Cupcakes

Chocolate Lava Cake

Ingredients:

- 4 ounces (115g) good quality dark chocolate
- 1/2 cup (115g) unsalted butter
- 1/2 cup (100g) granulated sugar
- 2 large eggs
- 2 large egg yolks
- 1 teaspoon vanilla extract
- 1/4 cup (30g) all-purpose flour
- Pinch of salt
- Optional: powdered sugar, cocoa powder, or vanilla ice cream for serving

Instructions:

1. Preheat your oven to 425°F (220°C). Grease and flour four ramekins or custard cups, ensuring they are well coated to prevent sticking.
2. In a heatproof bowl set over a pot of simmering water, melt the dark chocolate and unsalted butter together, stirring occasionally until smooth. Alternatively, you can melt them together in the microwave in short bursts, stirring between each burst until melted and smooth.
3. In a separate mixing bowl, whisk together the granulated sugar, eggs, egg yolks, and vanilla extract until well combined.
4. Gradually pour the melted chocolate mixture into the egg mixture, whisking constantly until smooth and well incorporated.
5. Sift the all-purpose flour and salt into the chocolate mixture, and gently fold them in until just combined. Be careful not to overmix.
6. Divide the batter evenly among the prepared ramekins, filling each about 3/4 full.
7. Place the filled ramekins on a baking sheet and transfer them to the preheated oven.
8. Bake for 12-14 minutes, or until the edges are set but the center still looks slightly soft and jiggly.
9. Carefully remove the lava cakes from the oven and let them cool for 1-2 minutes.
10. Using oven mitts or a kitchen towel, carefully invert each ramekin onto a serving plate to release the lava cake.
11. Dust the tops with powdered sugar or cocoa powder if desired, and serve immediately while still warm, optionally with a scoop of vanilla ice cream on the side.

Enjoy the rich and gooey center of these delicious Chocolate Lava Cakes!

Chocolate Mousse

Ingredients:

- 7 ounces (200g) good quality dark chocolate, chopped
- 3 large eggs, separated
- 1/4 cup (50g) granulated sugar
- 1 cup (240ml) heavy cream
- 1 teaspoon vanilla extract
- Pinch of salt
- Optional: whipped cream and chocolate shavings for garnish

Instructions:

1. Place the chopped dark chocolate in a heatproof bowl set over a pot of simmering water (double boiler). Stir the chocolate occasionally until melted and smooth. Alternatively, you can melt the chocolate in the microwave in short bursts, stirring between each burst until melted and smooth. Remove from heat and let it cool slightly.
2. In a large mixing bowl, beat the egg yolks with half of the granulated sugar until pale and creamy.
3. Gradually pour the melted chocolate into the egg yolk mixture, stirring constantly until well combined. Set aside.
4. In another clean mixing bowl, beat the egg whites with a pinch of salt until soft peaks form.
5. Gradually add the remaining granulated sugar to the egg whites while continuing to beat until stiff, glossy peaks form.
6. In a separate bowl, whip the heavy cream and vanilla extract until soft peaks form.
7. Gently fold the whipped cream into the chocolate mixture until well combined and no streaks remain.
8. Carefully fold the beaten egg whites into the chocolate mixture in two additions, folding gently until fully incorporated.
9. Divide the chocolate mousse evenly among serving glasses or bowls.
10. Cover and refrigerate the chocolate mousse for at least 2 hours, or until set.
11. Before serving, garnish with whipped cream and chocolate shavings if desired.

Enjoy the creamy and indulgent texture of this homemade Chocolate Mousse!

Chocolate Fondue

Ingredients:

- 8 ounces (225g) good quality dark chocolate, chopped
- 1/2 cup (120ml) heavy cream
- 1 tablespoon unsalted butter
- 1 teaspoon vanilla extract
- Assorted dippers: strawberries, bananas, pineapple, marshmallows, pretzels, pound cake, etc.

Instructions:

1. In a small saucepan, heat the heavy cream and unsalted butter over medium-low heat until it just starts to simmer.
2. Remove the saucepan from heat and add the chopped dark chocolate to the hot cream mixture.
3. Let the chocolate sit in the hot cream for a minute to soften, then stir gently until the chocolate is completely melted and the mixture is smooth and glossy.
4. Stir in the vanilla extract until well combined.
5. Transfer the chocolate fondue to a fondue pot or a serving bowl.
6. Light the fondue pot if using, following the manufacturer's instructions.
7. Arrange the assorted dippers on a platter or serving tray.
8. To serve, skewer a piece of fruit, marshmallow, or other dipper with a fondue fork or skewer, and dip it into the warm chocolate fondue, swirling to coat evenly.
9. Enjoy the delicious chocolate-coated dippers, and repeat with more dippers as desired.

Tip: If the chocolate fondue starts to thicken as it sits, you can reheat it gently over low heat or in short bursts in the microwave, stirring until smooth again.

Enjoy your chocolate fondue with friends and family for a fun and indulgent dessert experience!

Chocolate Truffles

Ingredients:

- 8 ounces (225g) good quality dark chocolate, chopped
- 1/2 cup (120ml) heavy cream
- 2 tablespoons unsalted butter, at room temperature
- 1 teaspoon vanilla extract
- Optional coatings: cocoa powder, powdered sugar, chopped nuts, shredded coconut, or melted chocolate

Instructions:

1. In a small saucepan, heat the heavy cream over medium heat until it just starts to simmer. Remove from heat.
2. Place the chopped dark chocolate in a heatproof bowl, and pour the hot cream over the chocolate. Let it sit for a minute to soften the chocolate.
3. Stir the chocolate and cream mixture together until smooth and well combined.
4. Add the unsalted butter and vanilla extract to the chocolate mixture, and stir until the butter is melted and fully incorporated.
5. Cover the bowl with plastic wrap and refrigerate the mixture for at least 2 hours, or until it is firm enough to handle and shape.
6. Once chilled, use a small spoon or a melon baller to scoop out portions of the chocolate mixture and roll them into small balls between your palms. Place the rolled truffles on a parchment-lined baking sheet.
7. If desired, roll the truffles in cocoa powder, powdered sugar, chopped nuts, shredded coconut, or dip them in melted chocolate for an extra layer of flavor and decoration.
8. Place the coated truffles back on the baking sheet and refrigerate them for another 15-30 minutes to set.
9. Once set, transfer the chocolate truffles to an airtight container and store them in the refrigerator until ready to serve.

Enjoy these homemade Chocolate Truffles as a decadent treat or give them as gifts to friends and family!

Chocolate Soufflé

Ingredients:

- 4 ounces (115g) good quality dark chocolate, chopped
- 3 tablespoons unsalted butter, plus extra for greasing ramekins
- 1/4 cup (50g) granulated sugar, plus extra for coating ramekins
- 3 large egg yolks
- 4 large egg whites
- Pinch of salt
- 1/4 teaspoon cream of tartar (optional, for stabilizing egg whites)
- Powdered sugar, for dusting (optional)
- Whipped cream or vanilla ice cream, for serving (optional)

Instructions:

1. Preheat your oven to 375°F (190°C). Grease the bottoms and sides of four 6-ounce (180ml) ramekins with butter, then coat them lightly with granulated sugar. Tap out any excess sugar.
2. In a heatproof bowl set over a pot of simmering water (double boiler), melt the dark chocolate and unsalted butter together, stirring occasionally until smooth. Remove from heat and let it cool slightly.
3. In a separate mixing bowl, whisk together the egg yolks and granulated sugar until pale and thick.
4. Gradually pour the melted chocolate mixture into the egg yolk mixture, whisking constantly until well combined.
5. In another clean mixing bowl, beat the egg whites with a pinch of salt (and cream of tartar, if using) until stiff peaks form.
6. Gently fold about one-third of the beaten egg whites into the chocolate mixture to lighten it.
7. Carefully fold the remaining egg whites into the chocolate mixture in two additions, folding gently until fully incorporated and no streaks remain.
8. Divide the soufflé batter evenly among the prepared ramekins, filling each about three-quarters full.
9. Smooth the tops of the soufflés with a spatula or the back of a spoon.
10. Place the filled ramekins on a baking sheet and transfer them to the preheated oven.

11. Bake the soufflés for 12-15 minutes, or until puffed up and set on top but still slightly jiggly in the center.
12. Remove the soufflés from the oven and dust the tops with powdered sugar if desired.
13. Serve the Chocolate Soufflés immediately, optionally with a dollop of whipped cream or a scoop of vanilla ice cream on the side.

Enjoy the light and airy texture of these delicious Chocolate Soufflés as a decadent dessert!

Chocolate Cheesecake

Ingredients:

For the crust:

- 1 1/2 cups (150g) chocolate cookie crumbs (from about 20 cookies)
- 1/4 cup (50g) granulated sugar
- 6 tablespoons (85g) unsalted butter, melted

For the filling:

- 24 ounces (680g) cream cheese, at room temperature
- 1 cup (200g) granulated sugar
- 1 cup (240ml) sour cream
- 3 large eggs
- 1 teaspoon vanilla extract
- 8 ounces (225g) good quality dark chocolate, melted and cooled slightly

Instructions:

1. Preheat your oven to 350°F (175°C). Wrap the bottom and sides of a 9-inch (23cm) springform pan with aluminum foil to prevent leaks. Grease the bottom and sides of the pan with butter or non-stick cooking spray.
2. In a mixing bowl, combine the chocolate cookie crumbs, granulated sugar, and melted butter. Stir until the crumbs are evenly moistened.
3. Press the crumb mixture into the bottom of the prepared springform pan, using the back of a spoon or the bottom of a glass to pack it down firmly.
4. Bake the crust in the preheated oven for 10 minutes. Remove from the oven and let it cool while you prepare the filling.
5. In a large mixing bowl, beat the cream cheese and granulated sugar together until smooth and creamy.
6. Add the sour cream, eggs, and vanilla extract to the cream cheese mixture, and beat until well combined and smooth.
7. Gradually pour the melted dark chocolate into the cream cheese mixture, beating continuously until fully incorporated and smooth.
8. Pour the chocolate cheesecake filling over the cooled crust in the springform pan, spreading it out evenly with a spatula.
9. Tap the filled pan gently on the counter a few times to release any air bubbles.

10. Place the springform pan in a larger baking dish or roasting pan, and pour hot water into the larger pan to create a water bath around the cheesecake.
11. Carefully transfer the water bath to the preheated oven and bake the cheesecake for 50-60 minutes, or until the edges are set but the center still jiggles slightly.
12. Turn off the oven and leave the cheesecake inside with the door closed for 1 hour to cool gradually.
13. After an hour, remove the cheesecake from the oven and let it cool to room temperature on a wire rack.
14. Once cooled, cover the cheesecake with plastic wrap and refrigerate it for at least 4 hours or overnight to set.
15. Before serving, carefully remove the sides of the springform pan. Slice and serve the Chocolate Cheesecake chilled, optionally topped with whipped cream, chocolate shavings, or fresh berries.

Enjoy the rich and creamy indulgence of this homemade Chocolate Cheesecake!

Chocolate Brownies

Ingredients:

- 1 cup (200g) granulated sugar
- 1/2 cup (115g) unsalted butter, melted
- 2 large eggs
- 1 teaspoon vanilla extract
- 1/3 cup (40g) unsweetened cocoa powder
- 1/2 cup (65g) all-purpose flour
- 1/4 teaspoon baking powder
- 1/4 teaspoon salt
- 1/2 cup (90g) chocolate chips or chopped chocolate (optional)

Instructions:

1. Preheat your oven to 350°F (175°C). Grease and flour an 8-inch (20cm) square baking pan, or line it with parchment paper for easy removal.
2. In a mixing bowl, combine the granulated sugar and melted butter. Stir until well combined.
3. Add the eggs and vanilla extract to the sugar-butter mixture, and whisk until smooth and creamy.
4. Sift the cocoa powder, all-purpose flour, baking powder, and salt into the wet ingredients. Stir until just combined and no lumps remain.
5. If using, fold in the chocolate chips or chopped chocolate until evenly distributed throughout the batter.
6. Pour the brownie batter into the prepared baking pan, spreading it out evenly with a spatula.
7. Bake the brownies in the preheated oven for 20-25 minutes, or until a toothpick inserted into the center comes out with a few moist crumbs attached.
8. Remove the brownies from the oven and let them cool completely in the pan on a wire rack.
9. Once cooled, use a sharp knife to cut the brownies into squares.
10. Serve the Chocolate Brownies as is or with a scoop of vanilla ice cream or a drizzle of chocolate sauce if desired.

Enjoy the rich, fudgy texture and indulgent chocolate flavor of these homemade Chocolate Brownies!

Chocolate Tiramisu

Ingredients:

- 1 cup (240ml) strong brewed coffee, cooled
- 1/4 cup (60ml) coffee liqueur (such as Kahlua), optional
- 2 tablespoons unsweetened cocoa powder
- 8 ounces (225g) mascarpone cheese, softened
- 1/2 cup (100g) granulated sugar
- 1 teaspoon vanilla extract
- 1 1/2 cups (360ml) heavy cream
- 24 ladyfinger cookies
- 4 ounces (115g) dark chocolate, grated or finely chopped

Instructions:

1. In a shallow dish, combine the cooled brewed coffee and coffee liqueur (if using). Set aside.
2. In a mixing bowl, sift the cocoa powder and set it aside.
3. In another mixing bowl, beat the softened mascarpone cheese, granulated sugar, and vanilla extract until smooth and creamy.
4. In a separate bowl, whip the heavy cream until stiff peaks form.
5. Gently fold the whipped cream into the mascarpone mixture until well combined and no streaks remain.
6. Dip each ladyfinger cookie into the coffee mixture briefly, making sure not to soak them too long, as they will become too soggy.
7. Arrange a layer of dipped ladyfinger cookies in the bottom of a serving dish or individual serving glasses.
8. Sprinkle half of the grated or chopped dark chocolate over the ladyfinger layer.
9. Spread half of the mascarpone mixture over the chocolate layer, smoothing it out evenly with a spatula.
10. Repeat the layers with the remaining dipped ladyfinger cookies, grated or chopped dark chocolate, and mascarpone mixture.
11. Cover the dish or glasses with plastic wrap and refrigerate the Chocolate Tiramisu for at least 4 hours, or overnight, to allow the flavors to meld and the dessert to set.
12. Before serving, dust the top of the tiramisu with the sifted cocoa powder for a finishing touch.

Enjoy the decadent and indulgent flavors of this homemade Chocolate Tiramisu!

Chocolate Silk Pie

Ingredients:

For the crust:

- 1 1/2 cups (about 180g) chocolate cookie crumbs (from about 20 cookies)
- 6 tablespoons (85g) unsalted butter, melted
- 1/4 cup (50g) granulated sugar

For the filling:

- 8 ounces (225g) good quality dark chocolate, chopped
- 1/2 cup (115g) unsalted butter, cut into pieces
- 1 cup (200g) granulated sugar
- 2 teaspoons vanilla extract
- 4 large eggs
- 1 cup (240ml) heavy cream
- Whipped cream and chocolate shavings for garnish (optional)

Instructions:

1. Preheat your oven to 350°F (175°C).
2. In a mixing bowl, combine the chocolate cookie crumbs, melted butter, and granulated sugar. Mix until well combined and the mixture resembles wet sand.
3. Press the mixture firmly into the bottom and up the sides of a 9-inch (23cm) pie dish to form the crust.
4. Bake the crust in the preheated oven for 10 minutes. Remove from the oven and let it cool completely on a wire rack.
5. In a heatproof bowl set over a pot of simmering water (double boiler), melt the chopped dark chocolate and unsalted butter together, stirring occasionally until smooth. Remove from heat and let it cool slightly.
6. In a separate mixing bowl, beat the granulated sugar, vanilla extract, and eggs together until light and fluffy.
7. Gradually pour the melted chocolate mixture into the egg mixture, whisking constantly until well combined.
8. In another mixing bowl, whip the heavy cream until stiff peaks form.
9. Gently fold the whipped cream into the chocolate mixture until smooth and well combined.

10. Pour the chocolate silk filling into the cooled pie crust, spreading it out evenly with a spatula.
11. Cover the pie with plastic wrap and refrigerate it for at least 4 hours, or until set.
12. Before serving, garnish the Chocolate Silk Pie with whipped cream and chocolate shavings if desired.

Enjoy the silky smooth texture and rich chocolate flavor of this decadent Chocolate Silk Pie!

Chocolate Covered Strawberries

Ingredients:

- 1 pound (about 450g) fresh strawberries, washed and dried thoroughly
- 8 ounces (225g) good quality dark or milk chocolate, chopped
- Optional toppings: chopped nuts, shredded coconut, sprinkles, or drizzled white chocolate

Instructions:

1. Line a baking sheet with parchment paper or wax paper.
2. Place the chopped chocolate in a heatproof bowl set over a pot of simmering water (double boiler).
3. Stir the chocolate occasionally until melted and smooth. Alternatively, you can melt the chocolate in the microwave in short bursts, stirring between each burst until melted and smooth.
4. Once the chocolate is melted, remove it from the heat and let it cool slightly for a few minutes.
5. Hold a strawberry by the stem and dip it into the melted chocolate, swirling to coat it evenly. Allow any excess chocolate to drip off.
6. If desired, roll the chocolate-covered strawberry in optional toppings like chopped nuts, shredded coconut, or sprinkles while the chocolate is still wet.
7. Place the dipped strawberries onto the prepared baking sheet, making sure they are not touching each other.
8. Repeat the dipping process with the remaining strawberries until they are all coated in chocolate.
9. If you have any leftover melted chocolate, you can drizzle it over the strawberries for an extra decorative touch.
10. Once all the strawberries are dipped and decorated, refrigerate them for about 15-20 minutes, or until the chocolate is set.
11. Once set, transfer the Chocolate Covered Strawberries to a serving platter or plate.
12. Serve the strawberries immediately, or store them in the refrigerator until ready to serve.

Enjoy these irresistible Chocolate Covered Strawberries as a sweet and indulgent treat!

Chocolate Banana Bread

Ingredients:

- 1 3/4 cups (220g) all-purpose flour
- 1/4 cup (25g) unsweetened cocoa powder
- 1 teaspoon baking powder
- 1/2 teaspoon baking soda
- 1/2 teaspoon salt
- 1/2 cup (115g) unsalted butter, softened
- 3/4 cup (150g) granulated sugar
- 2 large eggs
- 3 ripe bananas, mashed
- 1/3 cup (80ml) sour cream or Greek yogurt
- 1 teaspoon vanilla extract
- 1 cup (175g) semi-sweet chocolate chips or chopped chocolate

Instructions:

1. Preheat your oven to 350°F (175°C). Grease and flour a 9x5-inch (23x13cm) loaf pan or line it with parchment paper for easy removal.
2. In a mixing bowl, sift together the all-purpose flour, cocoa powder, baking powder, baking soda, and salt. Set aside.
3. In a separate mixing bowl, cream together the softened unsalted butter and granulated sugar until light and fluffy.
4. Add the eggs, one at a time, beating well after each addition.
5. Stir in the mashed bananas, sour cream or Greek yogurt, and vanilla extract until well combined.
6. Gradually add the dry ingredients to the wet ingredients, mixing until just combined and no streaks of flour remain.
7. Fold in the semi-sweet chocolate chips or chopped chocolate until evenly distributed throughout the batter.
8. Pour the batter into the prepared loaf pan, spreading it out evenly with a spatula.
9. Bake the Chocolate Banana Bread in the preheated oven for 50-60 minutes, or until a toothpick inserted into the center comes out clean or with a few moist crumbs.
10. Remove the bread from the oven and let it cool in the pan for 10-15 minutes.
11. Once cooled slightly, transfer the Chocolate Banana Bread to a wire rack to cool completely before slicing and serving.

Enjoy this moist and flavorful Chocolate Banana Bread as a delicious breakfast or snack!

Chocolate Chip Cookies

Ingredients:

- 1 cup (2 sticks or 225g) unsalted butter, softened
- 3/4 cup (150g) granulated sugar
- 3/4 cup (150g) packed brown sugar
- 2 large eggs
- 1 teaspoon vanilla extract
- 2 1/4 cups (280g) all-purpose flour
- 1 teaspoon baking soda
- 1/2 teaspoon salt
- 2 cups (340g) semi-sweet chocolate chips
- Optional: 1 cup (115g) chopped nuts such as walnuts or pecans

Instructions:

1. Preheat your oven to 375°F (190°C). Line baking sheets with parchment paper or silicone baking mats.
2. In a large mixing bowl, cream together the softened unsalted butter, granulated sugar, and brown sugar until light and fluffy.
3. Add the eggs one at a time, beating well after each addition. Then, stir in the vanilla extract until well combined.
4. In a separate mixing bowl, whisk together the all-purpose flour, baking soda, and salt.
5. Gradually add the dry ingredients to the wet ingredients, mixing until just combined. Be careful not to overmix.
6. Fold in the semi-sweet chocolate chips (and chopped nuts, if using) until evenly distributed throughout the cookie dough.
7. Drop rounded tablespoons of dough onto the prepared baking sheets, spacing them about 2 inches apart.
8. Bake the Chocolate Chip Cookies in the preheated oven for 9-11 minutes, or until the edges are lightly golden brown.
9. Remove the cookies from the oven and let them cool on the baking sheets for a few minutes before transferring them to wire racks to cool completely.

Enjoy these classic Chocolate Chip Cookies warm or at room temperature with a glass of milk for a comforting treat!

Chocolate Pudding

Ingredients:

- 1/2 cup (100g) granulated sugar
- 1/4 cup (30g) unsweetened cocoa powder
- 1/4 cup (30g) cornstarch
- Pinch of salt
- 2 1/2 cups (600ml) whole milk
- 2 large egg yolks
- 2 tablespoons (28g) unsalted butter
- 1 teaspoon vanilla extract
- Optional toppings: whipped cream, chocolate shavings, or fresh berries

Instructions:

1. In a medium saucepan, whisk together the granulated sugar, unsweetened cocoa powder, cornstarch, and salt until well combined.
2. Gradually whisk in the whole milk until smooth and no lumps remain.
3. Place the saucepan over medium heat and cook the mixture, stirring constantly with a whisk, until it thickens and comes to a boil. This should take about 5-7 minutes.
4. Once the mixture has thickened, continue to cook and whisk for another 1-2 minutes until it becomes very thick.
5. In a small bowl, whisk the egg yolks until smooth. Gradually whisk in about 1/2 cup of the hot pudding mixture into the egg yolks to temper them, whisking constantly.
6. Pour the tempered egg yolk mixture back into the saucepan with the remaining pudding mixture, whisking constantly.
7. Continue to cook the pudding for another 1-2 minutes, stirring constantly, until it thickens further.
8. Remove the saucepan from the heat and stir in the unsalted butter and vanilla extract until the butter is melted and the pudding is smooth and glossy.
9. Transfer the chocolate pudding to individual serving dishes or a large bowl.
10. Cover the surface of the pudding with plastic wrap to prevent a skin from forming, and refrigerate it for at least 2 hours, or until chilled and set.
11. Once chilled, serve the Chocolate Pudding cold, optionally topped with whipped cream, chocolate shavings, or fresh berries.

Enjoy the rich and creamy texture of this homemade Chocolate Pudding as a delicious dessert or snack!

Chocolate Eclairs

Ingredients:

For the choux pastry:

- 1/2 cup (120ml) water
- 1/2 cup (120ml) whole milk
- 1/2 cup (115g) unsalted butter, cut into small pieces
- 1 tablespoon granulated sugar
- 1/4 teaspoon salt
- 1 cup (125g) all-purpose flour
- 4 large eggs, at room temperature

For the filling:

- 1 1/2 cups (360ml) heavy cream
- 3 tablespoons powdered sugar
- 1 teaspoon vanilla extract

For the chocolate glaze:

- 4 ounces (115g) semisweet chocolate, chopped
- 1/2 cup (120ml) heavy cream
- 1 tablespoon unsalted butter

Instructions:

1. Preheat your oven to 400°F (200°C). Line a baking sheet with parchment paper or a silicone baking mat.
2. In a medium saucepan, combine the water, milk, butter, granulated sugar, and salt. Bring the mixture to a simmer over medium heat, stirring occasionally.
3. Once the mixture reaches a simmer and the butter has melted completely, add the all-purpose flour all at once. Stir vigorously with a wooden spoon until the mixture forms a smooth dough and pulls away from the sides of the pan.
4. Continue to cook the dough over low heat for 1-2 minutes to dry it out slightly. Stir constantly to prevent it from sticking to the bottom of the pan.
5. Transfer the dough to a mixing bowl and let it cool for a few minutes.
6. Add the eggs to the dough one at a time, mixing well after each addition, until the dough is smooth and glossy. It should be thick, but still able to fall off a spoon in a thick ribbon.

7. Transfer the choux pastry dough to a piping bag fitted with a large round tip (or simply cut off the corner of a plastic bag).
8. Pipe the dough onto the prepared baking sheet into 4-inch (10cm) long strips, leaving space between each eclair.
9. Bake the eclairs in the preheated oven for 15 minutes, then reduce the oven temperature to 350°F (180°C) and bake for an additional 20-25 minutes, or until golden brown and puffed up.
10. Remove the eclairs from the oven and let them cool completely on a wire rack.

For the filling:

1. In a mixing bowl, beat the heavy cream, powdered sugar, and vanilla extract together until stiff peaks form.
2. Transfer the whipped cream to a piping bag fitted with a small round tip.
3. Once the eclairs have cooled completely, use a sharp knife to cut a small slit in the side of each eclair.
4. Pipe the whipped cream filling into each eclair through the slit until they are filled.

For the chocolate glaze:

1. Place the chopped semisweet chocolate in a heatproof bowl.
2. In a small saucepan, heat the heavy cream and unsalted butter over medium heat until just simmering.
3. Pour the hot cream mixture over the chopped chocolate and let it sit for 1-2 minutes.
4. Stir the chocolate and cream together until smooth and glossy.
5. Let the chocolate glaze cool slightly before dipping the tops of the filled eclairs into it.
6. Place the dipped eclairs on a wire rack to allow any excess glaze to drip off.
7. Once the glaze has set, serve the Chocolate Eclairs immediately or store them in the refrigerator until ready to serve.

Enjoy the deliciously light and creamy Chocolate Eclairs as a decadent treat!

Chocolate Creme Brulee

Ingredients:

- 2 cups (480ml) heavy cream
- 4 ounces (115g) good quality dark chocolate, chopped
- 6 large egg yolks
- 1/2 cup (100g) granulated sugar, plus extra for caramelizing
- 1 teaspoon vanilla extract
- Pinch of salt
- Hot water for the water bath

Instructions:

1. Preheat your oven to 325°F (160°C). Place six ramekins in a baking dish large enough to hold them without touching each other.
2. In a medium saucepan, heat the heavy cream over medium heat until it just starts to simmer. Remove from heat and add the chopped dark chocolate to the hot cream. Let it sit for a minute to soften, then stir until the chocolate is completely melted and the mixture is smooth. Set aside to cool slightly.
3. In a separate mixing bowl, whisk together the egg yolks, granulated sugar, vanilla extract, and salt until well combined and slightly thickened.
4. Gradually pour the melted chocolate mixture into the egg yolk mixture, whisking constantly until smooth and well incorporated.
5. Strain the custard mixture through a fine-mesh sieve into a pouring jug to remove any lumps or air bubbles.
6. Divide the custard evenly among the ramekins. Fill the baking dish with hot water until it reaches about halfway up the sides of the ramekins, creating a water bath.
7. Carefully transfer the baking dish to the preheated oven and bake the crème brûlées for 30-35 minutes, or until the edges are set but the centers still have a slight jiggle.
8. Remove the baking dish from the oven and let the crème brûlées cool in the water bath for 10 minutes.
9. Carefully remove the ramekins from the water bath and transfer them to a wire rack to cool completely. Once cooled, cover the ramekins with plastic wrap and refrigerate them for at least 4 hours, or overnight, to set.

10. Before serving, sprinkle a thin, even layer of granulated sugar over the surface of each crème brûlée. Use a kitchen torch to caramelize the sugar until it forms a golden-brown crust.
11. Allow the caramelized sugar to cool and harden for a minute or two before serving.
12. Serve the Chocolate Crème Brûlée immediately, and enjoy the rich and creamy texture contrasted with the crackling caramelized sugar on top.

Chocolate Coconut Macaroons

Ingredients:

- 3 cups (270g) sweetened shredded coconut
- 2/3 cup (80g) unsweetened cocoa powder
- 1/2 cup (100g) granulated sugar
- 1/4 teaspoon salt
- 3 large egg whites
- 1 teaspoon vanilla extract
- 4 ounces (115g) semi-sweet chocolate, chopped (optional)
- Additional melted chocolate for drizzling (optional)

Instructions:

1. Preheat your oven to 325°F (160°C). Line a baking sheet with parchment paper or a silicone baking mat.
2. In a large mixing bowl, combine the sweetened shredded coconut, unsweetened cocoa powder, granulated sugar, and salt. Stir until well combined.
3. In a separate mixing bowl, beat the egg whites and vanilla extract together until stiff peaks form.
4. Gently fold the beaten egg whites into the coconut mixture until evenly combined. Be careful not to deflate the egg whites too much.
5. If using, fold in the chopped semi-sweet chocolate until evenly distributed throughout the mixture.
6. Using a spoon or a cookie scoop, portion out the coconut mixture and place mounds onto the prepared baking sheet, spacing them about 1 inch (2.5cm) apart.
7. Bake the chocolate coconut macaroons in the preheated oven for 15-18 minutes, or until the edges are firm and the tops are set.
8. Remove the baking sheet from the oven and let the macaroons cool on the baking sheet for a few minutes before transferring them to a wire rack to cool completely.
9. If desired, drizzle melted chocolate over the cooled macaroons for an extra touch of sweetness and decoration.
10. Let the chocolate drizzle set before serving or storing the Chocolate Coconut Macaroons in an airtight container at room temperature.

Enjoy these deliciously chocolatey and coconutty treats as a delightful snack or dessert!

Chocolate Raspberry Tart

Ingredients:

For the crust:

- 1 1/2 cups (180g) all-purpose flour
- 1/4 cup (50g) granulated sugar
- 1/4 teaspoon salt
- 1/2 cup (115g) unsalted butter, cold and cut into small cubes
- 1 large egg yolk
- 1-2 tablespoons ice water

For the chocolate ganache filling:

- 8 ounces (225g) semi-sweet chocolate, chopped
- 1 cup (240ml) heavy cream
- 1 tablespoon unsalted butter
- 1 teaspoon vanilla extract

For the raspberry topping:

- 2 cups (about 250g) fresh raspberries
- 2 tablespoons seedless raspberry jam, melted

Instructions:

1. Preheat your oven to 375°F (190°C). Grease a 9-inch (23cm) tart pan with a removable bottom.
2. In a food processor, combine the all-purpose flour, granulated sugar, and salt. Pulse to mix.
3. Add the cold cubed butter to the flour mixture and pulse until the mixture resembles coarse crumbs.
4. Add the egg yolk and pulse until the dough starts to come together.
5. Gradually add the ice water, 1 tablespoon at a time, and pulse until the dough forms a ball. Be careful not to overwork the dough.
6. Press the dough evenly into the bottom and up the sides of the prepared tart pan.

7. Prick the bottom of the crust with a fork and place the tart pan in the freezer for about 15 minutes to chill.
8. Once chilled, bake the crust in the preheated oven for 15-20 minutes, or until lightly golden brown. Remove from the oven and let it cool completely on a wire rack.
9. While the crust is cooling, prepare the chocolate ganache filling. Place the chopped semi-sweet chocolate in a heatproof bowl.
10. In a small saucepan, heat the heavy cream and unsalted butter over medium heat until it just starts to simmer.
11. Pour the hot cream mixture over the chopped chocolate and let it sit for 1-2 minutes.
12. Stir the chocolate and cream together until smooth and glossy. Stir in the vanilla extract until well combined.
13. Pour the chocolate ganache filling into the cooled tart crust and spread it out evenly with a spatula. Let it set at room temperature for about 30 minutes, or until slightly firm.
14. Arrange the fresh raspberries on top of the set chocolate ganache filling.
15. Brush the melted seedless raspberry jam over the raspberries to glaze them and add shine.
16. Refrigerate the Chocolate Raspberry Tart for at least 1 hour, or until the ganache is fully set.
17. Once set, remove the tart from the refrigerator, slice, and serve.

Enjoy the decadent combination of chocolate and raspberries in this delicious Chocolate Raspberry Tart!

Chocolate Peanut Butter Cups

Ingredients:

- 12 ounces (340g) semi-sweet chocolate, chopped
- 1/2 cup (125g) creamy peanut butter
- 1/4 cup (50g) powdered sugar
- 1/2 teaspoon vanilla extract
- Pinch of salt

Instructions:

1. Line a muffin tin with paper or silicone cupcake liners.
2. Place the chopped semi-sweet chocolate in a heatproof bowl. Microwave in 30-second intervals, stirring in between each interval, until the chocolate is melted and smooth. Alternatively, you can melt the chocolate using a double boiler.
3. Spoon a small amount of melted chocolate into the bottom of each cupcake liner, spreading it out to cover the bottom.
4. Place the muffin tin in the freezer for about 10 minutes to set the chocolate.
5. While the chocolate is setting, prepare the peanut butter filling. In a mixing bowl, combine the creamy peanut butter, powdered sugar, vanilla extract, and a pinch of salt. Stir until smooth and well combined.
6. Once the chocolate in the muffin tin has set, remove it from the freezer. Spoon a small amount of the peanut butter mixture on top of the set chocolate layer in each cupcake liner, pressing it down gently to flatten.
7. Pour the remaining melted chocolate over the peanut butter filling, covering it completely and smoothing the tops with a spoon.
8. Return the muffin tin to the freezer and let the Chocolate Peanut Butter Cups set for about 30 minutes, or until firm.
9. Once set, remove the Chocolate Peanut Butter Cups from the muffin tin and peel off the cupcake liners.
10. Serve the Chocolate Peanut Butter Cups immediately, or store them in an airtight container in the refrigerator until ready to serve.

Enjoy these homemade Chocolate Peanut Butter Cups as a delicious and satisfying treat!

Chocolate Cherry Trifle

Ingredients:

- 1 box (about 18 ounces or 510g) chocolate cake mix, prepared according to package instructions and cooled
- 2 cups (480ml) heavy cream
- 1/4 cup (30g) powdered sugar
- 1 teaspoon vanilla extract
- 1 can (about 21 ounces or 595g) cherry pie filling
- 1/2 cup (120ml) cherry liqueur or cherry juice (optional)
- Chocolate shavings or grated chocolate for garnish (optional)

Instructions:

1. Prepare the chocolate cake according to the package instructions. Once baked, allow it to cool completely.
2. While the cake is cooling, prepare the whipped cream. In a mixing bowl, beat the heavy cream, powdered sugar, and vanilla extract together until stiff peaks form. Set aside.
3. Once the cake has cooled, cut it into small cubes.
4. In a trifle dish or a large glass bowl, layer half of the chocolate cake cubes at the bottom.
5. If using, drizzle half of the cherry liqueur or cherry juice over the cake cubes.
6. Spoon half of the cherry pie filling over the cake cubes, spreading it out evenly.
7. Dollop half of the whipped cream over the cherry pie filling and spread it out into an even layer.
8. Repeat the layers with the remaining chocolate cake cubes, cherry liqueur or juice, cherry pie filling, and whipped cream.
9. If desired, garnish the top of the trifle with chocolate shavings or grated chocolate.
10. Cover the trifle dish with plastic wrap and refrigerate for at least 4 hours, or overnight, to allow the flavors to meld and the trifle to set.
11. Before serving, remove the trifle from the refrigerator and let it sit at room temperature for about 10-15 minutes.
12. Serve the Chocolate Cherry Trifle chilled and enjoy the layers of rich chocolate cake, sweet cherry filling, and creamy whipped cream.

This Chocolate Cherry Trifle is sure to be a hit at any gathering with its decadent layers and delicious flavors!

Chocolate Caramel Slice

Ingredients:

For the base:

- 1 cup (125g) all-purpose flour
- 1/2 cup (100g) granulated sugar
- 1/4 teaspoon salt
- 1/2 cup (115g) unsalted butter, melted

For the caramel filling:

- 1 can (14 ounces or 397g) sweetened condensed milk
- 1/2 cup (100g) brown sugar
- 1/4 cup (60g) unsalted butter
- 2 tablespoons golden syrup or light corn syrup
- 1 teaspoon vanilla extract

For the chocolate topping:

- 6 ounces (170g) semi-sweet chocolate, chopped
- 2 tablespoons (30g) unsalted butter

Instructions:

1. Preheat your oven to 350°F (175°C). Grease and line a 9x9-inch (23x23cm) square baking pan with parchment paper, leaving an overhang on the sides for easy removal.
2. In a mixing bowl, combine the all-purpose flour, granulated sugar, and salt. Add the melted unsalted butter and mix until well combined and the mixture resembles coarse crumbs.
3. Press the mixture evenly into the bottom of the prepared baking pan. Bake in the preheated oven for 12-15 minutes, or until lightly golden brown. Remove from the oven and let it cool slightly.
4. While the base is cooling, prepare the caramel filling. In a medium saucepan, combine the sweetened condensed milk, brown sugar, unsalted butter, and golden syrup or light corn syrup. Cook over medium heat, stirring constantly, until

the mixture thickens and turns a caramel color. This should take about 8-10 minutes.
5. Remove the caramel mixture from the heat and stir in the vanilla extract. Pour the caramel filling over the cooled base, spreading it out evenly with a spatula. Return the pan to the oven and bake for an additional 10-12 minutes, or until the caramel is set and slightly golden.
6. Remove the pan from the oven and let it cool completely on a wire rack.
7. Once the caramel slice has cooled, prepare the chocolate topping. In a heatproof bowl set over a pot of simmering water (double boiler), melt the chopped semi-sweet chocolate and unsalted butter together, stirring until smooth and glossy.
8. Pour the melted chocolate mixture over the cooled caramel filling, spreading it out evenly with a spatula.
9. Place the pan in the refrigerator for about 1-2 hours, or until the chocolate topping is set.
10. Once set, remove the chocolate caramel slice from the pan using the parchment paper overhang and transfer it to a cutting board. Cut it into squares or bars.
11. Serve the Chocolate Caramel Slice chilled or at room temperature.

Enjoy the irresistible combination of buttery base, gooey caramel filling, and rich chocolate topping in this decadent treat!

Chocolate Hazelnut Tart

Ingredients:

For the crust:

- 1 1/4 cups (155g) all-purpose flour
- 1/4 cup (30g) powdered sugar
- 1/4 teaspoon salt
- 1/2 cup (115g) unsalted butter, cold and cut into small cubes
- 1 large egg yolk
- 1-2 tablespoons ice water

For the filling:

- 1 cup (240ml) heavy cream
- 8 ounces (225g) semi-sweet chocolate, chopped
- 1/2 cup (120ml) hazelnut spread (such as Nutella)
- 1 teaspoon vanilla extract
- Pinch of salt

For the topping:

- 1/2 cup (75g) hazelnuts, toasted and chopped
- 2 tablespoons chocolate shavings or grated chocolate

Instructions:

1. Preheat your oven to 350°F (175°C). Grease a 9-inch (23cm) tart pan with a removable bottom.
2. In a food processor, combine the all-purpose flour, powdered sugar, and salt. Pulse to mix.
3. Add the cold cubed butter to the flour mixture and pulse until the mixture resembles coarse crumbs.
4. Add the egg yolk and pulse until the dough starts to come together.
5. Gradually add the ice water, 1 tablespoon at a time, and pulse until the dough forms a ball. Be careful not to overwork the dough.
6. Press the dough evenly into the bottom and up the sides of the prepared tart pan.

7. Prick the bottom of the crust with a fork and place the tart pan in the freezer for about 15 minutes to chill.
8. Once chilled, bake the crust in the preheated oven for 15-20 minutes, or until lightly golden brown. Remove from the oven and let it cool completely on a wire rack.
9. While the crust is cooling, prepare the filling. In a small saucepan, heat the heavy cream over medium heat until it just starts to simmer.
10. Place the chopped semi-sweet chocolate in a heatproof bowl. Pour the hot cream over the chocolate and let it sit for 1-2 minutes.
11. Stir the chocolate and cream together until smooth and glossy. Stir in the hazelnut spread, vanilla extract, and a pinch of salt until well combined.
12. Pour the chocolate hazelnut filling into the cooled tart crust and spread it out evenly with a spatula.
13. Sprinkle the toasted and chopped hazelnuts over the top of the filling.
14. Place the tart in the refrigerator for at least 1 hour, or until the filling is set.
15. Once set, remove the tart from the refrigerator and sprinkle the chocolate shavings or grated chocolate over the top.
16. Serve the Chocolate Hazelnut Tart chilled and enjoy the rich and nutty flavors!

This Chocolate Hazelnut Tart is sure to impress with its decadent chocolate filling and crunchy hazelnut topping.

Chocolate Peppermint Bark

Ingredients:

- 12 ounces (340g) semi-sweet chocolate, chopped
- 12 ounces (340g) white chocolate, chopped
- 1/2 teaspoon peppermint extract (divided)
- 1/2 cup (60g) crushed candy canes or peppermint candies

Instructions:

1. Line a baking sheet with parchment paper or a silicone baking mat.
2. In separate heatproof bowls, melt the semi-sweet chocolate and white chocolate. You can do this using a double boiler or by microwaving in 30-second intervals, stirring between each interval, until melted and smooth.
3. Once melted, stir 1/4 teaspoon of peppermint extract into each bowl of melted chocolate until well combined.
4. Pour the melted semi-sweet chocolate onto the prepared baking sheet and spread it out into an even layer with a spatula.
5. Next, pour the melted white chocolate over the semi-sweet chocolate layer and spread it out evenly.
6. While the chocolate is still wet, sprinkle the crushed candy canes or peppermint candies over the top, pressing them down gently into the chocolate.
7. Place the baking sheet in the refrigerator for about 1 hour, or until the chocolate is completely set and firm.
8. Once set, remove the bark from the refrigerator and break it into pieces using your hands or a knife.
9. Store the Chocolate Peppermint Bark in an airtight container at room temperature or in the refrigerator until ready to serve.

Enjoy the sweet and refreshing combination of chocolate and peppermint in this festive treat!

Chocolate Bread Pudding

Ingredients:

- 6 cups (about 12 ounces or 340g) day-old bread, cut into cubes (such as French bread or brioche)
- 2 cups (480ml) whole milk
- 1 cup (240ml) heavy cream
- 3/4 cup (150g) granulated sugar
- 4 large eggs
- 1/4 cup (25g) unsweetened cocoa powder
- 1 teaspoon vanilla extract
- 1/2 teaspoon ground cinnamon
- 1/4 teaspoon salt
- 1 cup (175g) semi-sweet chocolate chips or chopped chocolate
- Optional: powdered sugar, whipped cream, or vanilla ice cream for serving

Instructions:

1. Preheat your oven to 350°F (175°C). Grease a 9x13-inch (23x33cm) baking dish with butter or cooking spray.
2. Place the bread cubes in the prepared baking dish, spreading them out evenly.
3. In a medium saucepan, heat the whole milk, heavy cream, and granulated sugar over medium heat until just simmering, stirring occasionally to dissolve the sugar. Remove from heat and let it cool slightly.
4. In a mixing bowl, whisk together the eggs, unsweetened cocoa powder, vanilla extract, ground cinnamon, and salt until well combined.
5. Gradually whisk the warm milk mixture into the egg mixture until smooth and well incorporated.
6. Pour the custard mixture over the bread cubes in the baking dish, making sure to coat them evenly. Let it sit for about 10-15 minutes to allow the bread to absorb the custard.
7. Sprinkle the semi-sweet chocolate chips or chopped chocolate over the top of the bread pudding.
8. Place the baking dish in the preheated oven and bake for 35-40 minutes, or until the bread pudding is set and the top is golden brown.
9. Remove the bread pudding from the oven and let it cool slightly before serving.

10. Serve the Chocolate Bread Pudding warm, optionally dusted with powdered sugar and topped with whipped cream or vanilla ice cream.

Enjoy the rich and comforting flavors of this Chocolate Bread Pudding as a delicious dessert or indulgent breakfast treat!

Chocolate Marshmallow Bars

Ingredients:

- 1/2 cup (115g) unsalted butter
- 1 cup (200g) granulated sugar
- 2 large eggs
- 1 teaspoon vanilla extract
- 1/3 cup (40g) unsweetened cocoa powder
- 1/2 cup (65g) all-purpose flour
- 1/4 teaspoon salt
- 1/4 teaspoon baking powder
- 2 cups (about 50 large) marshmallows
- 1 cup (175g) semi-sweet chocolate chips

Instructions:

1. Preheat your oven to 350°F (175°C). Grease an 8x8-inch (20x20cm) baking pan or line it with parchment paper.
2. In a medium saucepan, melt the unsalted butter over low heat.
3. Remove the saucepan from the heat and stir in the granulated sugar until well combined.
4. Beat in the eggs, one at a time, until incorporated.
5. Stir in the vanilla extract.
6. In a separate bowl, sift together the unsweetened cocoa powder, all-purpose flour, salt, and baking powder.
7. Gradually add the dry ingredients to the wet ingredients, mixing until just combined.
8. Spread the batter evenly into the prepared baking pan.
9. Bake in the preheated oven for 20-25 minutes, or until a toothpick inserted into the center comes out with moist crumbs but no wet batter.
10. Remove the pan from the oven and immediately sprinkle the marshmallows evenly over the top of the hot bars.
11. Return the pan to the oven and bake for an additional 2-3 minutes, or until the marshmallows are puffed and golden brown.
12. Remove the pan from the oven and let it cool on a wire rack.

13. While the bars are cooling, melt the semi-sweet chocolate chips in a microwave-safe bowl in 30-second intervals, stirring between each interval, until smooth and melted.
14. Once the bars have cooled slightly, drizzle the melted chocolate over the top.
15. Let the bars cool completely in the pan before cutting them into squares.

Enjoy these irresistible Chocolate Marshmallow Bars as a sweet and gooey treat!

Chocolate Orange Cake

Ingredients:

For the cake:

- 1 3/4 cups (220g) all-purpose flour
- 3/4 cup (75g) unsweetened cocoa powder
- 1 1/2 teaspoons baking powder
- 1 1/2 teaspoons baking soda
- 1/2 teaspoon salt
- 1 1/2 cups (300g) granulated sugar
- 2 large eggs
- 1 cup (240ml) orange juice (freshly squeezed if possible)
- 1/2 cup (120ml) vegetable oil
- 1 tablespoon orange zest
- 1 teaspoon vanilla extract

For the chocolate orange ganache:

- 6 ounces (170g) semi-sweet chocolate, chopped
- 1/2 cup (120ml) heavy cream
- 2 tablespoons unsalted butter
- 1 tablespoon orange zest

For the orange syrup (optional):

- 1/4 cup (60ml) orange juice
- 2 tablespoons granulated sugar

Instructions:

1. Preheat your oven to 350°F (175°C). Grease and flour two 9-inch (23cm) round cake pans.
2. In a large mixing bowl, sift together the all-purpose flour, unsweetened cocoa powder, baking powder, baking soda, and salt.
3. In another mixing bowl, whisk together the granulated sugar and eggs until well combined.
4. Add the orange juice, vegetable oil, orange zest, and vanilla extract to the sugar and egg mixture, and whisk until smooth.

5. Gradually add the dry ingredients to the wet ingredients, stirring until just combined and no lumps remain. Be careful not to overmix.
6. Divide the batter evenly between the prepared cake pans and smooth the tops with a spatula.
7. Bake in the preheated oven for 25-30 minutes, or until a toothpick inserted into the center of the cakes comes out clean.
8. Remove the cakes from the oven and let them cool in the pans for 10 minutes before transferring them to a wire rack to cool completely.

For the chocolate orange ganache:

1. In a heatproof bowl, combine the chopped semi-sweet chocolate and orange zest.
2. In a small saucepan, heat the heavy cream and unsalted butter over medium heat until it just starts to simmer.
3. Pour the hot cream mixture over the chopped chocolate and orange zest. Let it sit for 1-2 minutes.
4. Stir the mixture until smooth and glossy. Let it cool slightly before using.

For the orange syrup (optional):

1. In a small saucepan, combine the orange juice and granulated sugar.
2. Heat over medium heat, stirring constantly, until the sugar is dissolved and the mixture is slightly thickened.
3. Remove from heat and let it cool completely.

To assemble:

1. Place one of the cooled cakes on a serving plate or cake stand.
2. If using, brush the top of the cake with the orange syrup.
3. Spread a layer of chocolate orange ganache over the top of the cake.
4. Place the second cake on top and press down gently.
5. Spread the remaining chocolate orange ganache over the top and sides of the cake, using a spatula to create swirls or patterns if desired.
6. Refrigerate the cake for at least 30 minutes to allow the ganache to set.
7. Once set, slice and serve the Chocolate Orange Cake.

Enjoy the rich chocolate flavor with a hint of citrus in this delightful Chocolate Orange Cake!

Chocolate Almond Biscotti

Ingredients:

- 2 cups (250g) all-purpose flour
- 1/2 cup (50g) unsweetened cocoa powder
- 1 teaspoon baking powder
- 1/4 teaspoon salt
- 1/2 cup (115g) unsalted butter, softened
- 1 cup (200g) granulated sugar
- 2 large eggs
- 1 teaspoon vanilla extract
- 1 cup (125g) almonds, toasted and coarsely chopped
- 1 cup (175g) semi-sweet chocolate chips

Instructions:

1. Preheat your oven to 350°F (175°C). Line a baking sheet with parchment paper.
2. In a medium bowl, whisk together the all-purpose flour, unsweetened cocoa powder, baking powder, and salt. Set aside.
3. In a large mixing bowl, cream together the softened unsalted butter and granulated sugar until light and fluffy.
4. Beat in the eggs, one at a time, until well combined. Stir in the vanilla extract.
5. Gradually add the dry ingredients to the wet ingredients, mixing until a stiff dough forms.
6. Fold in the toasted and chopped almonds and semi-sweet chocolate chips until evenly distributed throughout the dough.
7. Divide the dough in half. On a lightly floured surface, shape each half into a log about 12 inches (30cm) long and 2 inches (5cm) wide. Place the logs onto the prepared baking sheet, leaving space between them.
8. Bake in the preheated oven for 25-30 minutes, or until the logs are firm to the touch and slightly cracked on top.
9. Remove the baking sheet from the oven and let the logs cool for 10-15 minutes. Reduce the oven temperature to 325°F (160°C).
10. Using a sharp knife, slice the logs diagonally into 1/2-inch (1.25cm) thick slices. Arrange the slices cut side down on the baking sheet.
11. Bake the biscotti slices for an additional 10-12 minutes, or until crisp and dry. Remove from the oven and let them cool completely on a wire rack.

12. Once cooled, store the Chocolate Almond Biscotti in an airtight container at room temperature.

Enjoy these crunchy and chocolatey biscotti with a cup of coffee or tea for a delightful treat!

Chocolate Cream Pie

Ingredients:

For the crust:

- 1 1/2 cups (190g) chocolate cookie crumbs (about 25-30 cookies)
- 6 tablespoons (85g) unsalted butter, melted

For the filling:

- 1/2 cup (100g) granulated sugar
- 1/4 cup (30g) cornstarch
- 1/4 teaspoon salt
- 4 large egg yolks
- 2 cups (480ml) whole milk
- 6 ounces (170g) semi-sweet chocolate, chopped
- 1 teaspoon vanilla extract

For the whipped cream topping:

- 1 cup (240ml) heavy cream
- 2 tablespoons powdered sugar
- 1/2 teaspoon vanilla extract

Instructions:

1. Preheat your oven to 350°F (175°C).
2. In a medium bowl, mix together the chocolate cookie crumbs and melted unsalted butter until well combined.
3. Press the mixture firmly into the bottom and up the sides of a 9-inch (23cm) pie dish to form the crust.
4. Bake the crust in the preheated oven for 10-12 minutes, or until set. Remove from the oven and let it cool completely on a wire rack.
5. In a medium saucepan, whisk together the granulated sugar, cornstarch, and salt.
6. In a separate bowl, whisk together the egg yolks and whole milk until well combined.
7. Gradually whisk the egg mixture into the sugar mixture until smooth.

8. Place the saucepan over medium heat and cook, stirring constantly, until the mixture thickens and comes to a boil. This should take about 5-7 minutes.
9. Remove the saucepan from the heat and stir in the chopped semi-sweet chocolate and vanilla extract until the chocolate is melted and the mixture is smooth.
10. Pour the filling into the cooled crust and smooth the top with a spatula. Cover the pie with plastic wrap, pressing it directly onto the surface of the filling to prevent a skin from forming.
11. Refrigerate the pie for at least 4 hours, or until set.
12. Before serving, prepare the whipped cream topping. In a mixing bowl, beat the heavy cream, powdered sugar, and vanilla extract together until stiff peaks form.
13. Spread the whipped cream over the chilled pie.
14. Optionally, garnish the pie with chocolate shavings or grated chocolate.
15. Slice and serve the Chocolate Cream Pie chilled.

Enjoy this rich and creamy chocolate pie as a decadent dessert for any occasion!

Chocolate Toffee Crunch

Ingredients:

- 1 cup (2 sticks or 225g) unsalted butter
- 1 cup (200g) granulated sugar
- 1/4 cup (60ml) water
- 1/2 teaspoon salt
- 1 teaspoon vanilla extract
- 12 ounces (340g) semi-sweet chocolate, chopped
- 1 cup (175g) chopped toasted almonds or pecans (optional)

Instructions:

1. Line a baking sheet with parchment paper or a silicone baking mat.
2. In a medium saucepan, combine the unsalted butter, granulated sugar, water, and salt over medium heat.
3. Stir the mixture constantly until the butter is melted and the sugar is dissolved.
4. Once the mixture comes to a boil, continue to cook it, stirring occasionally, until it reaches 300°F (150°C) on a candy thermometer. This should take about 10-15 minutes.
5. Remove the saucepan from the heat and stir in the vanilla extract.
6. Carefully pour the hot toffee mixture onto the prepared baking sheet, spreading it out into an even layer with a spatula.
7. Let the toffee cool and harden completely at room temperature. This will take about 1-2 hours.
8. Once the toffee is completely cooled and hardened, melt the semi-sweet chocolate in a microwave-safe bowl in 30-second intervals, stirring between each interval, until smooth and melted.
9. Pour the melted chocolate over the cooled toffee layer, spreading it out evenly with a spatula.
10. Sprinkle the chopped toasted almonds or pecans over the melted chocolate layer, pressing them down gently into the chocolate.
11. Place the baking sheet in the refrigerator for about 30 minutes, or until the chocolate is set.
12. Once set, remove the Chocolate Toffee Crunch from the refrigerator and break it into pieces using your hands or a knife.

13. Store the Chocolate Toffee Crunch in an airtight container at room temperature or in the refrigerator until ready to serve.

Enjoy the sweet and crunchy goodness of this Chocolate Toffee Crunch as a delicious snack or homemade gift!

Chocolate Dipped Pretzels

Ingredients:

- Pretzel rods or mini pretzels
- 8 ounces (225g) semi-sweet chocolate, chopped
- 8 ounces (225g) white chocolate, chopped (optional)
- Assorted toppings: chopped nuts, sprinkles, crushed candy canes, etc. (optional)

Instructions:

1. Line a baking sheet with parchment paper or wax paper.
2. In separate microwave-safe bowls, melt the semi-sweet chocolate and white chocolate in 30-second intervals, stirring between each interval, until smooth and melted.
3. Dip each pretzel rod or mini pretzel into the melted chocolate, coating it halfway or fully, depending on your preference.
4. Use a fork or dipping tool to shake off any excess chocolate from the pretzel.
5. Place the chocolate-dipped pretzels onto the prepared baking sheet.
6. If desired, sprinkle the dipped pretzels with assorted toppings while the chocolate is still wet.
7. Repeat the dipping process with the remaining pretzels.
8. Once all the pretzels are dipped and decorated, let them sit at room temperature or place them in the refrigerator for about 10-15 minutes to allow the chocolate to set.
9. Once set, the Chocolate Dipped Pretzels are ready to serve.

Enjoy these sweet and salty treats as a delicious snack or homemade gift!

Chocolate Rice Krispie Treats

Ingredients:

- 6 cups (about 150g) crispy rice cereal (such as Rice Krispies)
- 4 cups (about 240g) mini marshmallows
- 3 tablespoons (42g) unsalted butter
- 1/2 cup (90g) semi-sweet chocolate chips
- 1/2 teaspoon vanilla extract
- Pinch of salt

Instructions:

1. Grease a 9x13-inch (23x33cm) baking pan or line it with parchment paper.
2. In a large saucepan, melt the unsalted butter over low heat.
3. Add the mini marshmallows to the melted butter and stir until completely melted and smooth.
4. Once the marshmallows are melted, remove the saucepan from the heat and stir in the semi-sweet chocolate chips until melted and smooth.
5. Stir in the vanilla extract and a pinch of salt.
6. Add the crispy rice cereal to the marshmallow mixture and stir until evenly coated.
7. Quickly transfer the mixture to the prepared baking pan and press it down firmly into an even layer using a greased spatula or your hands.
8. Let the Chocolate Rice Krispie Treats cool at room temperature for about 30 minutes, or until set.
9. Once set, cut the treats into squares using a sharp knife.
10. Serve and enjoy the Chocolate Rice Krispie Treats as a delicious snack or dessert!

These treats are perfect for satisfying your sweet tooth and are sure to be a hit with kids and adults alike!

Chocolate Strawberry Shortcake

Ingredients:

For the shortcakes:

- 2 cups (250g) all-purpose flour
- 1/2 cup (100g) granulated sugar
- 1/4 cup (25g) unsweetened cocoa powder
- 1 tablespoon baking powder
- 1/2 teaspoon salt
- 1/2 cup (115g) cold unsalted butter, cut into small pieces
- 3/4 cup (180ml) heavy cream
- 1 teaspoon vanilla extract

For the strawberries:

- 1 pound (450g) fresh strawberries, hulled and sliced
- 2 tablespoons granulated sugar
- 1 tablespoon lemon juice

For the whipped cream:

- 1 cup (240ml) heavy cream
- 2 tablespoons powdered sugar
- 1 teaspoon vanilla extract

For garnish:

- Fresh whole strawberries
- Chocolate shavings or grated chocolate

Instructions:

1. Preheat your oven to 400°F (200°C). Line a baking sheet with parchment paper.
2. In a large mixing bowl, whisk together the flour, sugar, cocoa powder, baking powder, and salt.

3. Add the cold butter pieces to the flour mixture and using a pastry cutter or your fingers, cut the butter into the dry ingredients until the mixture resembles coarse crumbs.
4. In a separate bowl, mix together the heavy cream and vanilla extract.
5. Gradually add the cream mixture to the dry ingredients, stirring until the dough comes together.
6. Turn the dough out onto a lightly floured surface and gently knead it a few times until it forms a smooth ball.
7. Pat the dough into a circle about 3/4 inch (2cm) thick. Use a round cutter or a glass to cut out 6 rounds of dough. Place the rounds onto the prepared baking sheet.
8. Bake the shortcakes in the preheated oven for 15-18 minutes, or until they are set and lightly golden.
9. Remove from the oven and let them cool on a wire rack.
10. While the shortcakes are cooling, prepare the strawberries. In a bowl, toss the sliced strawberries with granulated sugar and lemon juice. Let them sit for about 15-20 minutes to release their juices.
11. In a separate bowl, prepare the whipped cream. Beat the heavy cream, powdered sugar, and vanilla extract together until stiff peaks form.
12. To assemble, slice each shortcake in half horizontally. Place a spoonful of strawberries on the bottom half, followed by a dollop of whipped cream. Place the other half of the shortcake on top.
13. Garnish with a whole strawberry and chocolate shavings or grated chocolate.
14. Serve immediately and enjoy this delightful Chocolate Strawberry Shortcake!

This dessert is perfect for any occasion and will surely impress your guests with its rich chocolate flavor and sweet strawberries.

Chocolate Pistachio Cake

Ingredients:

For the cake:

- 1 and 3/4 cups (220g) all-purpose flour
- 1 cup (200g) granulated sugar
- 3/4 cup (65g) unsweetened cocoa powder
- 1 and 1/2 teaspoons baking powder
- 1 and 1/2 teaspoons baking soda
- 1 teaspoon salt
- 2 large eggs, at room temperature
- 1 cup (240ml) whole milk, at room temperature
- 1/2 cup (120ml) vegetable oil
- 2 teaspoons vanilla extract
- 1 cup (240ml) boiling water

For the frosting:

- 1 cup (230g) unsalted butter, softened
- 3 and 1/2 cups (420g) powdered sugar, sifted
- 1/2 cup (50g) unsweetened cocoa powder
- 1/2 cup (120ml) heavy cream
- 1 teaspoon vanilla extract
- 1/2 cup (60g) chopped pistachios, plus extra for garnish

Instructions:

1. Preheat your oven to 350°F (175°C). Grease and flour two 9-inch (23cm) round cake pans and line the bottoms with parchment paper.
2. In a large mixing bowl, sift together the flour, sugar, cocoa powder, baking powder, baking soda, and salt.
3. Add the eggs, milk, vegetable oil, and vanilla extract to the dry ingredients. Beat on medium speed for 2 minutes until well combined.
4. Stir in the boiling water until the batter is smooth. The batter will be thin.
5. Divide the batter evenly between the prepared cake pans.

6. Bake in the preheated oven for 30-35 minutes, or until a toothpick inserted into the center of the cakes comes out clean.
7. Remove the cakes from the oven and allow them to cool in the pans for 10 minutes before transferring them to a wire rack to cool completely.
8. While the cakes are cooling, prepare the frosting. In a large mixing bowl, beat the softened butter until creamy.
9. Gradually add the sifted powdered sugar and cocoa powder, beating on low speed until well combined.
10. Gradually add the heavy cream and vanilla extract, beating on medium-high speed until light and fluffy.
11. Stir in the chopped pistachios.
12. Once the cakes are completely cooled, place one layer on a serving plate or cake stand. Spread a layer of frosting over the top.
13. Place the second layer of cake on top and frost the top and sides of the cake with the remaining frosting.
14. Garnish the top of the cake with additional chopped pistachios.
15. Slice and serve your delicious Chocolate Pistachio Cake!

Enjoy this decadent and flavorful cake, perfect for any special occasion or dessert table.

Chocolate Cinnamon Rolls

Ingredients:

For the dough:

- 1 cup (240ml) whole milk
- 1/4 cup (50g) granulated sugar
- 1/4 cup (60g) unsalted butter
- 1 package (2 and 1/4 teaspoons) active dry yeast
- 1 large egg
- 3 and 1/2 cups (440g) all-purpose flour, plus extra for dusting
- 1/2 teaspoon salt

For the filling:

- 1/2 cup (100g) brown sugar, packed
- 1/4 cup (25g) unsweetened cocoa powder
- 1 tablespoon ground cinnamon
- 1/4 cup (60g) unsalted butter, softened

For the glaze:

- 1 cup (120g) powdered sugar
- 2 tablespoons (30ml) milk
- 1/2 teaspoon vanilla extract

Instructions:

1. In a small saucepan, heat the milk, sugar, and butter over medium heat until the butter is melted and the mixture is warm (about 110°F or 45°C).
2. Transfer the warm milk mixture to a large mixing bowl and sprinkle the yeast over the top. Let it sit for about 5 minutes until the yeast is foamy.
3. Add the egg and stir to combine.
4. Gradually add the flour and salt to the yeast mixture, stirring until a soft dough forms.

5. Turn the dough out onto a lightly floured surface and knead for about 5-7 minutes until smooth and elastic.
6. Place the dough in a greased bowl, cover with a clean kitchen towel, and let it rise in a warm place for about 1 hour or until doubled in size.
7. Once the dough has risen, punch it down and roll it out into a large rectangle, about 1/4 inch (6mm) thick.
8. In a small bowl, mix together the brown sugar, cocoa powder, and cinnamon for the filling.
9. Spread the softened butter evenly over the surface of the dough, then sprinkle the brown sugar mixture over the butter.
10. Starting from one long edge, tightly roll up the dough into a log. Pinch the seam to seal.
11. Using a sharp knife or dental floss, cut the dough into 12 equal slices.
12. Place the rolls in a greased 9x13-inch (23x33cm) baking dish, cover with a clean kitchen towel, and let them rise for another 30 minutes.
13. Preheat your oven to 375°F (190°C).
14. Bake the rolls in the preheated oven for 20-25 minutes, or until golden brown and cooked through.
15. While the rolls are baking, prepare the glaze by whisking together the powdered sugar, milk, and vanilla extract until smooth.
16. Once the rolls are done, remove them from the oven and let them cool for a few minutes before drizzling with the glaze.
17. Serve the Chocolate Cinnamon Rolls warm and enjoy!

These decadent rolls are perfect for breakfast or brunch, and the combination of chocolate and cinnamon is sure to be a hit with everyone!

Chocolate Macadamia Nut Cookies

Ingredients:

- 1 cup (2 sticks or 226g) unsalted butter, softened
- 1 cup (200g) granulated sugar
- 1 cup (220g) packed light brown sugar
- 2 large eggs
- 1 teaspoon vanilla extract
- 2 cups (250g) all-purpose flour
- 2/3 cup (80g) unsweetened cocoa powder
- 1 teaspoon baking soda
- 1/4 teaspoon salt
- 1 cup (150g) chopped macadamia nuts
- 1 cup (175g) semi-sweet chocolate chips

Instructions:

1. Preheat your oven to 350°F (175°C). Line baking sheets with parchment paper.
2. In a large mixing bowl, cream together the softened unsalted butter, granulated sugar, and brown sugar until light and fluffy.
3. Beat in the eggs, one at a time, until well combined. Stir in the vanilla extract.
4. In a separate bowl, sift together the all-purpose flour, cocoa powder, baking soda, and salt.
5. Gradually add the dry ingredients to the wet ingredients, mixing until just combined.
6. Fold in the chopped macadamia nuts and semi-sweet chocolate chips until evenly distributed throughout the dough.
7. Drop rounded tablespoons of dough onto the prepared baking sheets, spacing them about 2 inches apart.
8. Bake in the preheated oven for 10-12 minutes, or until the cookies are set around the edges but still soft in the center.
9. Remove from the oven and let the cookies cool on the baking sheets for a few minutes before transferring them to wire racks to cool completely.
10. Once cooled, store the Chocolate Macadamia Nut Cookies in an airtight container at room temperature.

Enjoy these delicious cookies with a glass of milk or your favorite hot beverage for a delightful treat!

Chocolate Peanut Butter Brownies

Ingredients:

For the brownie layer:

- 1/2 cup (115g) unsalted butter
- 1 cup (200g) granulated sugar
- 2 large eggs
- 1 teaspoon vanilla extract
- 1/3 cup (40g) unsweetened cocoa powder
- 1/2 cup (65g) all-purpose flour
- 1/4 teaspoon salt
- 1/4 teaspoon baking powder

For the peanut butter layer:

- 1/2 cup (125g) creamy peanut butter
- 1/4 cup (50g) granulated sugar
- 1 large egg
- 1/2 teaspoon vanilla extract

Instructions:

1. Preheat your oven to 350°F (175°C). Grease and flour an 8x8-inch (20x20cm) baking pan or line it with parchment paper.
2. In a medium saucepan, melt the unsalted butter over low heat.
3. Remove the saucepan from the heat and stir in the granulated sugar until well combined.
4. Beat in the eggs, one at a time, until incorporated. Stir in the vanilla extract.
5. In a separate bowl, sift together the unsweetened cocoa powder, all-purpose flour, salt, and baking powder.
6. Gradually add the dry ingredients to the wet ingredients, mixing until just combined.
7. Spread the brownie batter evenly into the prepared baking pan.
8. In another mixing bowl, beat together the creamy peanut butter, granulated sugar, egg, and vanilla extract until smooth.

9. Drop spoonfuls of the peanut butter mixture over the brownie batter in the pan.
10. Use a knife or spatula to swirl the peanut butter mixture into the brownie batter, creating a marbled effect.
11. Bake in the preheated oven for 25-30 minutes, or until a toothpick inserted into the center comes out with moist crumbs but no wet batter.
12. Remove the pan from the oven and let it cool completely on a wire rack.
13. Once cooled, slice the Chocolate Peanut Butter Brownies into squares and serve.

Enjoy the delicious combination of chocolate and peanut butter in these irresistible brownies!

Chocolate Espresso Cake

Ingredients:

For the cake:

- 1 and 3/4 cups (220g) all-purpose flour
- 3/4 cup (65g) unsweetened cocoa powder
- 1 and 3/4 cups (350g) granulated sugar
- 2 teaspoons baking soda
- 1 teaspoon baking powder
- 1 teaspoon salt
- 2 large eggs
- 1 cup (240ml) buttermilk
- 1 cup (240ml) strong brewed coffee, cooled
- 1/2 cup (120ml) vegetable oil
- 2 teaspoons vanilla extract

For the espresso buttercream frosting:

- 1 cup (2 sticks or 226g) unsalted butter, softened
- 3 and 1/2 cups (420g) powdered sugar, sifted
- 2 tablespoons instant espresso powder, dissolved in 2 tablespoons hot water
- 1 teaspoon vanilla extract
- Pinch of salt

For garnish (optional):

- Chocolate-covered espresso beans
- Cocoa powder

Instructions:

1. Preheat your oven to 350°F (175°C). Grease and flour two 9-inch (23cm) round cake pans and line the bottoms with parchment paper.
2. In a large mixing bowl, sift together the all-purpose flour, cocoa powder, granulated sugar, baking soda, baking powder, and salt.

3. In another mixing bowl, whisk together the eggs, buttermilk, cooled brewed coffee, vegetable oil, and vanilla extract until well combined.
4. Gradually add the wet ingredients to the dry ingredients, stirring until smooth and well combined.
5. Divide the batter evenly between the prepared cake pans.
6. Bake in the preheated oven for 25-30 minutes, or until a toothpick inserted into the center of the cakes comes out clean.
7. Remove the cakes from the oven and let them cool in the pans for 10 minutes before transferring them to wire racks to cool completely.
8. While the cakes are cooling, prepare the espresso buttercream frosting. In a large mixing bowl, beat the softened butter until creamy.
9. Gradually add the powdered sugar, beating on low speed until well combined.
10. Add the dissolved instant espresso powder, vanilla extract, and pinch of salt, and beat on medium-high speed until light and fluffy.
11. Once the cakes are completely cooled, place one layer on a serving plate or cake stand. Spread a layer of espresso buttercream frosting over the top.
12. Place the second layer of cake on top and frost the top and sides of the cake with the remaining frosting.
13. Garnish the top of the cake with chocolate-covered espresso beans and dust with cocoa powder if desired.
14. Slice and serve your delicious Chocolate Espresso Cake!

Enjoy the rich chocolate flavor and bold espresso kick in this indulgent cake, perfect for any special occasion or dessert table.

Chocolate Mint Ice Cream

Ingredients:

- 2 cups (480ml) heavy cream
- 1 cup (240ml) whole milk
- 3/4 cup (150g) granulated sugar
- 1/4 teaspoon salt
- 1 teaspoon peppermint extract
- 1/2 teaspoon vanilla extract
- Green food coloring (optional)
- 1 cup (175g) semi-sweet chocolate chips or chunks, chopped

Instructions:

1. In a medium saucepan, combine the heavy cream, whole milk, granulated sugar, and salt. Heat the mixture over medium heat, stirring occasionally, until the sugar is dissolved and the mixture is warm.
2. Remove the saucepan from the heat and stir in the peppermint extract and vanilla extract. If desired, add a few drops of green food coloring to achieve the desired mint color.
3. Cover the saucepan and refrigerate the mixture until thoroughly chilled, at least 2-3 hours or overnight.
4. Once the mixture is chilled, pour it into an ice cream maker and churn according to the manufacturer's instructions until it reaches a soft-serve consistency.
5. In the last few minutes of churning, add the chopped semi-sweet chocolate chips or chunks and continue churning until evenly distributed.
6. Transfer the churned ice cream to a freezer-safe container and freeze for at least 4 hours or until firm.
7. Serve the Chocolate Mint Ice Cream scoops in bowls or cones, and enjoy!

This refreshing and creamy ice cream with a hint of mint and chocolate is perfect for cooling off on a hot day or as a delightful dessert anytime.

Chocolate Coconut Pudding

Ingredients:
- 2 cups (480ml) canned coconut milk
- 1/3 cup (65g) granulated sugar
- 1/4 cup (20g) unsweetened cocoa powder
- 2 tablespoons (16g) cornstarch
- 1/4 teaspoon salt
- 1 teaspoon vanilla extract
- Shredded coconut, for garnish (optional)

Instructions:

1. In a medium saucepan, whisk together the canned coconut milk, granulated sugar, unsweetened cocoa powder, cornstarch, and salt until well combined and smooth.
2. Place the saucepan over medium heat and cook the mixture, stirring constantly, until it thickens and begins to bubble. This should take about 5-7 minutes.
3. Once the pudding has thickened, remove the saucepan from the heat and stir in the vanilla extract.
4. Divide the pudding evenly among serving dishes or glasses.
5. Cover the surface of each pudding with plastic wrap to prevent a skin from forming. Place the pudding dishes in the refrigerator and chill for at least 2 hours, or until set.
6. Before serving, optionally garnish each pudding with shredded coconut.
7. Serve the Chocolate Coconut Pudding chilled and enjoy its creamy texture and rich chocolate-coconut flavor!

This pudding is a delightful treat for any chocolate and coconut lover, and it's easy to make with just a few simple ingredients.

Chocolate Walnut Fudge

Ingredients:

- 3 cups (540g) semi-sweet chocolate chips
- 1 can (14 ounces or 396g) sweetened condensed milk
- 1/4 cup (55g) unsalted butter
- 1 teaspoon vanilla extract
- 1 cup (120g) chopped walnuts

Instructions:

1. Line an 8x8-inch (20x20cm) square baking pan with parchment paper or aluminum foil, leaving some overhang for easy removal. Grease the paper or foil lightly with butter or non-stick cooking spray.
2. In a medium saucepan, combine the semi-sweet chocolate chips, sweetened condensed milk, and unsalted butter over low heat.
3. Stir the mixture continuously until the chocolate chips and butter are melted and the mixture is smooth and well combined.
4. Remove the saucepan from the heat and stir in the vanilla extract and chopped walnuts until evenly distributed throughout the fudge mixture.
5. Pour the fudge mixture into the prepared baking pan and spread it out evenly using a spatula.
6. Optionally, you can press additional chopped walnuts on top of the fudge for decoration.
7. Let the fudge cool at room temperature for about 30 minutes, then transfer it to the refrigerator to chill for at least 2 hours, or until firm.
8. Once the fudge is firm, lift it out of the pan using the parchment paper or foil overhang and place it on a cutting board.
9. Use a sharp knife to cut the fudge into squares of your desired size.
10. Serve and enjoy the delicious Chocolate Walnut Fudge!

This rich and indulgent fudge is perfect for satisfying your sweet tooth or for gifting to friends and family during the holidays or special occasions. Store any leftover fudge in an airtight container in the refrigerator for up to two weeks.

Chocolate Caramel Macarons

Ingredients:

For the macaron shells:

- 1 cup (100g) almond flour
- 1 cup (100g) powdered sugar
- 2 large egg whites, at room temperature
- 1/4 cup (50g) granulated sugar
- 1/4 teaspoon cream of tartar
- 1/4 teaspoon salt
- 1/2 teaspoon vanilla extract
- 2 tablespoons unsweetened cocoa powder

For the caramel filling:

- 1/2 cup (100g) granulated sugar
- 2 tablespoons water
- 1/4 cup (60ml) heavy cream
- 2 tablespoons unsalted butter
- 1/4 teaspoon salt
- 1/2 teaspoon vanilla extract

Instructions:

1. Preheat your oven to 300°F (150°C). Line two baking sheets with parchment paper.
2. In a food processor, combine the almond flour, powdered sugar, and cocoa powder. Pulse until well combined and fine in texture. Sift the mixture into a large mixing bowl to remove any lumps.
3. In a separate mixing bowl, beat the egg whites on medium speed until foamy. Add the cream of tartar and continue beating until soft peaks form.
4. Gradually add the granulated sugar and salt while continuing to beat. Increase the speed to high and beat until stiff peaks form.
5. Add the vanilla extract and beat until incorporated.

6. Gently fold the sifted almond flour mixture into the egg white mixture in three additions, until the batter is smooth and forms ribbons when lifted with a spatula.
7. Transfer the batter to a piping bag fitted with a round tip.
8. Pipe small circles (about 1 inch or 2.5 cm in diameter) onto the prepared baking sheets, spacing them about 1 inch apart.
9. Tap the baking sheets firmly against the counter to release any air bubbles. Let the piped macarons sit at room temperature for about 30 minutes to form a skin.
10. Bake the macarons in the preheated oven for 15-18 minutes, or until they are set and can be easily lifted off the parchment paper. Let them cool completely on the baking sheets.
11. While the macarons are cooling, prepare the caramel filling. In a small saucepan, combine the granulated sugar and water over medium heat. Cook, stirring occasionally, until the sugar is dissolved.
12. Once the sugar is dissolved, stop stirring and let the mixture come to a boil. Continue to cook, swirling the pan occasionally, until the caramel turns a deep amber color.
13. Remove the saucepan from the heat and carefully add the heavy cream, butter, salt, and vanilla extract. Be cautious as the mixture may bubble up.
14. Return the saucepan to low heat and cook, stirring constantly, until the caramel is smooth and thickened, about 2-3 minutes. Remove from heat and let cool slightly.
15. Pair the cooled macaron shells by size.
16. Spoon a small amount of caramel filling onto the flat side of one macaron shell and sandwich with another shell. Repeat with the remaining macaron shells.
17. Place the filled macarons in an airtight container and refrigerate for at least 24 hours before serving to allow the flavors to meld.
18. Serve and enjoy these delicious Chocolate Caramel Macarons!

These macarons are sure to impress with their rich chocolate flavor and gooey caramel filling. They make a perfect treat for special occasions or as a gift for friends and family.

Chocolate Bourbon Pecan Pie

Ingredients:

For the crust:

- 1 and 1/4 cups (155g) all-purpose flour
- 1/2 teaspoon salt
- 1/2 teaspoon granulated sugar
- 1/2 cup (115g) unsalted butter, cold and cut into small pieces
- 3-4 tablespoons ice water

For the filling:

- 1 cup (200g) granulated sugar
- 3 large eggs
- 1 cup (240ml) dark corn syrup
- 2 tablespoons bourbon whiskey
- 1 teaspoon vanilla extract
- 2 tablespoons unsalted butter, melted
- 1 cup (120g) pecan halves
- 1/2 cup (85g) semi-sweet chocolate chips

Instructions:

1. To make the crust, combine the all-purpose flour, salt, and granulated sugar in a large mixing bowl. Add the cold butter pieces and use a pastry cutter or fork to cut the butter into the flour mixture until it resembles coarse crumbs.
2. Gradually add the ice water, 1 tablespoon at a time, mixing with a fork until the dough just holds together when squeezed with your fingers.
3. Shape the dough into a disk, wrap it in plastic wrap, and refrigerate for at least 1 hour.
4. Preheat your oven to 375°F (190°C). On a lightly floured surface, roll out the chilled dough into a circle large enough to fit into a 9-inch (23cm) pie dish. Transfer the dough to the pie dish, trim any excess overhang, and crimp the edges. Place the pie dish in the refrigerator while you prepare the filling.

5. In a large mixing bowl, whisk together the granulated sugar and eggs until well combined.
6. Add the dark corn syrup, bourbon whiskey, vanilla extract, and melted butter, and whisk until smooth.
7. Stir in the pecan halves and semi-sweet chocolate chips until evenly distributed.
8. Pour the filling into the prepared pie crust.
9. Place the pie on a baking sheet to catch any spills, and bake in the preheated oven for 40-50 minutes, or until the filling is set and the crust is golden brown.
10. Remove the pie from the oven and let it cool completely on a wire rack before slicing and serving.
11. Serve the Chocolate Bourbon Pecan Pie at room temperature, optionally topped with whipped cream or a scoop of vanilla ice cream.
12. Enjoy this decadent and flavorful pie with its perfect balance of chocolate, bourbon, and pecans!

This Chocolate Bourbon Pecan Pie is a delicious twist on the classic pecan pie, making it an impressive dessert for holidays or special occasions.

Chocolate Cherry Clafoutis

Ingredients:

- 1 cup (240ml) whole milk
- 1/2 cup (120ml) heavy cream
- 1/2 cup (100g) granulated sugar
- 3 large eggs
- 1 teaspoon vanilla extract
- 1/4 teaspoon almond extract (optional)
- 1/2 cup (60g) all-purpose flour
- 1/4 cup (25g) unsweetened cocoa powder
- 1/4 teaspoon salt
- 1 and 1/2 cups (225g) fresh cherries, pitted
- Powdered sugar, for dusting (optional)

Instructions:

1. Preheat your oven to 350°F (175°C). Grease a 9-inch (23cm) pie dish or cast iron skillet.
2. In a medium saucepan, heat the whole milk, heavy cream, and granulated sugar over medium heat until the sugar is dissolved and the mixture is warm. Remove from heat and let it cool slightly.
3. In a large mixing bowl, whisk together the eggs, vanilla extract, and almond extract (if using) until well combined.
4. In a separate bowl, sift together the all-purpose flour, cocoa powder, and salt.
5. Gradually add the dry ingredients to the egg mixture, whisking until smooth.
6. Gradually pour the warm milk mixture into the batter, whisking continuously until well combined and smooth.
7. Arrange the pitted cherries in the greased pie dish or skillet.
8. Pour the batter over the cherries, covering them evenly.
9. Bake in the preheated oven for 35-40 minutes, or until the clafoutis is set and the top is puffed and slightly golden.
10. Remove from the oven and let it cool for a few minutes before serving.
11. Dust with powdered sugar before serving if desired.
12. Serve the Chocolate Cherry Clafoutis warm or at room temperature, and enjoy!

This Chocolate Cherry Clafoutis is a delightful dessert that combines the rich flavor of chocolate with the sweet tartness of fresh cherries. It's perfect for any occasion and sure to impress your guests!

Chocolate Custard Tart

Ingredients:

For the crust:

- 1 and 1/4 cups (155g) all-purpose flour
- 1/4 cup (30g) unsweetened cocoa powder
- 1/4 cup (50g) granulated sugar
- 1/2 cup (115g) unsalted butter, cold and cut into small pieces
- 1 large egg yolk
- 2 tablespoons ice water

For the chocolate custard filling:

- 2 cups (480ml) whole milk
- 1/2 cup (100g) granulated sugar
- 1/4 cup (30g) cornstarch
- 1/4 cup (25g) unsweetened cocoa powder
- 4 large egg yolks
- 6 ounces (170g) semi-sweet chocolate, chopped
- 1 teaspoon vanilla extract

Instructions:

1. To make the crust, combine the all-purpose flour, cocoa powder, and granulated sugar in a food processor. Add the cold butter pieces and pulse until the mixture resembles coarse crumbs.
2. Add the egg yolk and ice water, and pulse until the dough comes together.
3. Turn the dough out onto a lightly floured surface and knead gently until smooth. Shape the dough into a disk, wrap it in plastic wrap, and refrigerate for at least 30 minutes.
4. Preheat your oven to 375°F (190°C). Roll out the chilled dough on a lightly floured surface into a circle large enough to fit into a 9-inch (23cm) tart pan. Press the dough into the bottom and up the sides of the tart pan. Trim any excess dough.
5. Line the crust with parchment paper and fill it with pie weights or dried beans. Bake for 15 minutes. Remove the parchment paper and weights, and bake for an

additional 10 minutes, or until the crust is set and dry. Remove from the oven and let it cool.
6. To make the chocolate custard filling, in a medium saucepan, whisk together the whole milk, granulated sugar, cornstarch, cocoa powder, and egg yolks until smooth.
7. Place the saucepan over medium heat and cook, stirring constantly, until the mixture thickens and comes to a boil.
8. Remove the saucepan from the heat and stir in the chopped semi-sweet chocolate and vanilla extract until the chocolate is melted and the mixture is smooth.
9. Pour the chocolate custard filling into the cooled tart crust and spread it out evenly.
10. Refrigerate the tart for at least 2 hours, or until the filling is set.
11. Serve the Chocolate Custard Tart chilled, optionally garnished with whipped cream or fresh berries.
12. Enjoy this decadent and rich chocolate dessert!

This Chocolate Custard Tart is perfect for any chocolate lover and makes a stunning dessert for special occasions or gatherings.

Chocolate Hazelnut Biscotti

Ingredients:

- 1 and 3/4 cups (220g) all-purpose flour
- 1/2 cup (50g) unsweetened cocoa powder
- 1 teaspoon baking powder
- 1/4 teaspoon salt
- 1/2 cup (115g) unsalted butter, softened
- 3/4 cup (150g) granulated sugar
- 2 large eggs
- 1 teaspoon vanilla extract
- 1/2 cup (60g) hazelnuts, toasted and chopped
- 1/2 cup (90g) semi-sweet chocolate chips or chunks

Instructions:

1. Preheat your oven to 350°F (175°C). Line a baking sheet with parchment paper or a silicone baking mat.
2. In a medium bowl, whisk together the all-purpose flour, cocoa powder, baking powder, and salt. Set aside.
3. In a large mixing bowl, cream together the softened unsalted butter and granulated sugar until light and fluffy.
4. Beat in the eggs, one at a time, until well combined. Stir in the vanilla extract.
5. Gradually add the dry ingredients to the wet ingredients, mixing until just combined.
6. Fold in the chopped hazelnuts and semi-sweet chocolate chips or chunks until evenly distributed throughout the dough.
7. Divide the dough in half. Shape each half into a log about 12 inches (30cm) long and 2 inches (5cm) wide, and place them on the prepared baking sheet, spaced a few inches apart.
8. Flatten the logs slightly with your hands or a spatula to about 1/2 inch (1.5cm) thickness.
9. Bake in the preheated oven for 25-30 minutes, or until the logs are set and slightly firm to the touch.
10. Remove the baking sheet from the oven and let the logs cool for about 10 minutes. Reduce the oven temperature to 325°F (160°C).
11. Using a sharp knife, carefully slice the logs diagonally into 1/2 inch (1.5cm) thick slices.

12. Place the biscotti slices cut side down on the baking sheet and bake for an additional 10-12 minutes, or until the biscotti are dry and crisp.
13. Remove from the oven and let the biscotti cool completely on a wire rack.
14. Once cooled, store the Chocolate Hazelnut Biscotti in an airtight container at room temperature.
15. Enjoy these delicious biscotti with a cup of coffee or tea for a delightful treat!

These Chocolate Hazelnut Biscotti are crunchy, chocolaty, and packed with nutty flavor, making them the perfect accompaniment to your morning or afternoon beverage.

Chocolate Raspberry Cheesecake

Ingredients:

For the crust:

- 1 and 1/2 cups (150g) chocolate cookie crumbs (such as Oreos)
- 1/4 cup (50g) granulated sugar
- 6 tablespoons (85g) unsalted butter, melted

For the cheesecake filling:

- 24 ounces (680g) cream cheese, softened
- 1 cup (200g) granulated sugar
- 3 large eggs
- 1 cup (240ml) sour cream
- 1 teaspoon vanilla extract
- 6 ounces (170g) semi-sweet chocolate, melted and cooled slightly

For the raspberry swirl:

- 1 cup (125g) fresh raspberries
- 2 tablespoons granulated sugar

Instructions:

1. Preheat your oven to 325°F (160°C). Wrap the outside of a 9-inch (23cm) springform pan with aluminum foil to prevent any leaks.
2. In a medium bowl, combine the chocolate cookie crumbs, granulated sugar, and melted butter. Press the mixture evenly into the bottom of the prepared springform pan.
3. In a large mixing bowl, beat the softened cream cheese and granulated sugar until smooth and creamy.
4. Add the eggs, one at a time, beating well after each addition.
5. Mix in the sour cream and vanilla extract until smooth.
6. Pour half of the cheesecake batter over the crust in the springform pan.

7. Stir the melted semi-sweet chocolate into the remaining cheesecake batter until well combined.
8. Pour the chocolate cheesecake batter over the plain cheesecake layer in the pan.
9. In a small saucepan, combine the fresh raspberries and granulated sugar. Cook over medium heat, stirring frequently, until the raspberries break down and the mixture thickens slightly, about 5 minutes. Remove from heat and strain the mixture through a fine-mesh sieve to remove the seeds.
10. Drop spoonfuls of the raspberry sauce onto the surface of the cheesecake batter in the pan. Use a knife or skewer to swirl the raspberry sauce into the cheesecake batter to create a marbled effect.
11. Place the springform pan in a large roasting pan and fill the roasting pan with enough hot water to reach halfway up the sides of the springform pan.
12. Bake the cheesecake in the preheated oven for 55-65 minutes, or until the edges are set and the center is slightly jiggly.
13. Turn off the oven and leave the cheesecake inside with the door closed for 1 hour to cool gradually.
14. Remove the cheesecake from the oven and run a knife around the edges to loosen it from the pan. Allow it to cool completely at room temperature, then refrigerate for at least 4 hours or overnight before serving.
15. Slice and serve the Chocolate Raspberry Cheesecake chilled, optionally topped with whipped cream and fresh raspberries.

Enjoy this decadent and creamy cheesecake with the perfect combination of rich chocolate and tart raspberries!

Chocolate Pecan Pie Bars

Ingredients:

For the crust:

- 1 and 1/2 cups (190g) all-purpose flour
- 1/2 cup (110g) unsalted butter, softened
- 1/4 cup (50g) granulated sugar
- 1/4 teaspoon salt

For the pecan filling:

- 1 cup (200g) dark corn syrup
- 3/4 cup (150g) granulated sugar
- 3 large eggs
- 2 tablespoons unsalted butter, melted
- 1 teaspoon vanilla extract
- 1 and 1/2 cups (180g) chopped pecans
- 1 cup (175g) semi-sweet chocolate chips

Instructions:

1. Preheat your oven to 350°F (175°C). Grease a 9x13-inch (23x33cm) baking pan or line it with parchment paper, leaving some overhang for easy removal.
2. In a mixing bowl, cream together the softened unsalted butter, granulated sugar, and salt until light and fluffy.
3. Gradually add the all-purpose flour, mixing until a dough forms.
4. Press the dough evenly into the bottom of the prepared baking pan.
5. Bake the crust in the preheated oven for 15-18 minutes, or until lightly golden. Remove from the oven and let it cool slightly.
6. In a separate mixing bowl, whisk together the dark corn syrup, granulated sugar, eggs, melted unsalted butter, and vanilla extract until well combined.
7. Stir in the chopped pecans and semi-sweet chocolate chips until evenly distributed.
8. Pour the pecan filling over the partially baked crust, spreading it out evenly.

9. Return the pan to the oven and bake for an additional 25-30 minutes, or until the filling is set and the edges are golden brown.
10. Remove from the oven and let the bars cool completely in the pan on a wire rack.
11. Once cooled, use a sharp knife to cut the bars into squares or rectangles.
12. Serve and enjoy these delicious Chocolate Pecan Pie Bars!

These bars are perfect for satisfying your sweet tooth with their rich chocolate, nutty pecan, and gooey filling. They're great for parties, gatherings, or as a special treat for yourself!

Chocolate Toffee Trifle

Ingredients:

- 1 package (3.9 ounces) instant chocolate pudding mix
- 2 cups cold milk
- 1 cup heavy cream
- 2 tablespoons powdered sugar
- 1 teaspoon vanilla extract
- 1 store-bought pound cake or homemade chocolate cake, cut into cubes
- 1 cup toffee bits or chopped toffee bars
- Chocolate sauce, for drizzling (optional)

Instructions:

1. In a large mixing bowl, whisk together the instant chocolate pudding mix and cold milk until thickened. Place the pudding in the refrigerator to set while you prepare the other components.
2. In another mixing bowl, whip the heavy cream with powdered sugar and vanilla extract until stiff peaks form. Set aside.
3. In a trifle dish or a large glass bowl, layer half of the chocolate cake cubes on the bottom.
4. Spoon half of the prepared chocolate pudding over the cake layer, spreading it out evenly.
5. Sprinkle half of the toffee bits over the pudding layer.
6. Next, layer the remaining chocolate cake cubes on top of the toffee bits.
7. Spoon the remaining chocolate pudding over the cake layer, spreading it out evenly.
8. Sprinkle the remaining toffee bits over the pudding layer.
9. Finally, spread the whipped cream over the top of the trifle, covering the toffee bits completely.
10. Optionally, drizzle chocolate sauce over the top of the whipped cream for an extra chocolatey touch.
11. Chill the Chocolate Toffee Trifle in the refrigerator for at least 1-2 hours before serving to allow the flavors to meld and the dessert to set.
12. Serve and enjoy this deliciously decadent dessert!

This Chocolate Toffee Trifle is sure to impress with its layers of rich chocolate pudding, fluffy whipped cream, and crunchy toffee bits. It's perfect for special occasions or any time you're craving a sweet treat!

Chocolate Gingerbread Cake

Ingredients:

- 1 and 3/4 cups (220g) all-purpose flour
- 1/2 cup (50g) unsweetened cocoa powder
- 1 teaspoon baking powder
- 1/2 teaspoon baking soda
- 1 teaspoon ground cinnamon
- 1 teaspoon ground ginger
- 1/4 teaspoon ground cloves
- 1/4 teaspoon salt
- 1/2 cup (115g) unsalted butter, softened
- 1/2 cup (100g) granulated sugar
- 1/2 cup (100g) packed light brown sugar
- 2 large eggs
- 1 teaspoon vanilla extract
- 1/2 cup (120ml) molasses
- 3/4 cup (180ml) hot water

Instructions:

1. Preheat your oven to 350°F (175°C). Grease and flour a 9-inch (23cm) round cake pan or line it with parchment paper.
2. In a medium bowl, whisk together the all-purpose flour, cocoa powder, baking powder, baking soda, ground cinnamon, ground ginger, ground cloves, and salt. Set aside.
3. In a large mixing bowl, cream together the softened unsalted butter, granulated sugar, and light brown sugar until light and fluffy.
4. Add the eggs, one at a time, beating well after each addition. Stir in the vanilla extract.
5. Gradually add the molasses to the butter mixture, mixing until well combined.
6. Gradually add the dry ingredients to the wet ingredients, alternating with the hot water, beginning and ending with the dry ingredients. Mix until just combined, being careful not to overmix.
7. Pour the batter into the prepared cake pan and spread it out evenly.
8. Bake in the preheated oven for 30-35 minutes, or until a toothpick inserted into the center of the cake comes out clean.

9. Remove the cake from the oven and let it cool in the pan for 10 minutes before transferring it to a wire rack to cool completely.
10. Once cooled, you can dust the Chocolate Gingerbread Cake with powdered sugar or frost it with your favorite frosting, such as cream cheese frosting or chocolate ganache, if desired.
11. Slice and serve the cake, and enjoy its rich, spicy, and chocolaty flavor!

This Chocolate Gingerbread Cake is perfect for holiday gatherings or any time you're craving a festive and indulgent dessert. Its combination of warm spices and rich chocolate makes it a delightful treat for chocolate lovers and gingerbread enthusiasts alike!

Chocolate Caramel Cheesecake

Ingredients:

For the crust:

- 1 and 1/2 cups (150g) chocolate cookie crumbs (such as Oreos)
- 1/4 cup (50g) granulated sugar
- 6 tablespoons (85g) unsalted butter, melted

For the cheesecake filling:

- 24 ounces (680g) cream cheese, softened
- 1 cup (200g) granulated sugar
- 3 large eggs
- 1 teaspoon vanilla extract
- 1/2 cup (120ml) heavy cream
- 4 ounces (113g) semi-sweet chocolate, melted and cooled slightly

For the caramel sauce:

- 1 cup (200g) granulated sugar
- 6 tablespoons (85g) unsalted butter, cut into pieces
- 1/2 cup (120ml) heavy cream
- 1 teaspoon vanilla extract
- Pinch of salt

Instructions:

1. Preheat your oven to 350°F (175°C). Grease a 9-inch (23cm) springform pan and wrap the outside with aluminum foil to prevent leaks.
2. In a mixing bowl, combine the chocolate cookie crumbs, granulated sugar, and melted butter. Press the mixture evenly into the bottom of the prepared springform pan. Bake the crust in the preheated oven for 10 minutes. Remove from the oven and let it cool while preparing the filling.
3. In a large mixing bowl, beat the softened cream cheese and granulated sugar until smooth and creamy.

4. Add the eggs, one at a time, beating well after each addition. Stir in the vanilla extract.
5. Gradually add the heavy cream and mix until smooth.
6. Fold in the melted semi-sweet chocolate until well combined.
7. Pour the cheesecake filling over the cooled crust and spread it out evenly.
8. Place the springform pan in a large roasting pan and fill the roasting pan with enough hot water to reach halfway up the sides of the springform pan.
9. Bake the cheesecake in the preheated oven for 50-60 minutes, or until the edges are set and the center is slightly jiggly.
10. Turn off the oven and leave the cheesecake inside with the door closed for 1 hour to cool gradually.
11. Remove the cheesecake from the oven and refrigerate it for at least 4 hours or overnight to set.
12. While the cheesecake is chilling, prepare the caramel sauce. In a medium saucepan, heat the granulated sugar over medium heat, stirring constantly with a wooden spoon or heatproof spatula until it melts and turns amber in color.
13. Carefully add the butter, stirring constantly until melted and combined.
14. Slowly pour in the heavy cream while stirring constantly. Be cautious as the mixture may bubble up.
15. Remove the caramel sauce from the heat and stir in the vanilla extract and salt.
16. Let the caramel sauce cool slightly before drizzling it over the chilled cheesecake.
17. Return the cheesecake to the refrigerator to allow the caramel sauce to set for at least 30 minutes before serving.
18. Slice and serve the Chocolate Caramel Cheesecake, optionally garnishing with whipped cream, chocolate shavings, or additional caramel sauce.
19. Enjoy this decadent and indulgent dessert!

This Chocolate Caramel Cheesecake is rich, creamy, and packed with irresistible flavors.

It's perfect for special occasions or anytime you're craving a luxurious treat!

Chocolate Blueberry Cupcakes

Ingredients:

For the cupcakes:

- 1 and 1/2 cups (190g) all-purpose flour
- 1/2 cup (50g) unsweetened cocoa powder
- 1 teaspoon baking powder
- 1/2 teaspoon baking soda
- 1/4 teaspoon salt
- 1/2 cup (120ml) vegetable oil
- 1 cup (200g) granulated sugar
- 2 large eggs
- 1 teaspoon vanilla extract
- 1/2 cup (120ml) buttermilk
- 1 cup (150g) fresh blueberries

For the chocolate ganache frosting:

- 6 ounces (170g) semi-sweet chocolate, chopped
- 1/2 cup (120ml) heavy cream

For garnish (optional):

- Fresh blueberries

Instructions:

1. Preheat your oven to 350°F (175°C). Line a muffin tin with cupcake liners.
2. In a medium bowl, sift together the all-purpose flour, cocoa powder, baking powder, baking soda, and salt. Set aside.
3. In a large mixing bowl, whisk together the vegetable oil and granulated sugar until well combined.
4. Add the eggs one at a time, beating well after each addition. Stir in the vanilla extract.

5. Gradually add the dry ingredients to the wet ingredients, alternating with the buttermilk, beginning and ending with the dry ingredients. Mix until just combined.
6. Gently fold in the fresh blueberries until evenly distributed throughout the batter.
7. Divide the batter evenly among the prepared cupcake liners, filling each about 2/3 full.
8. Bake in the preheated oven for 18-20 minutes, or until a toothpick inserted into the center of a cupcake comes out clean.
9. Remove the cupcakes from the oven and let them cool in the muffin tin for 5 minutes before transferring them to a wire rack to cool completely.
10. While the cupcakes are cooling, prepare the chocolate ganache frosting. Place the chopped semi-sweet chocolate in a heatproof bowl.
11. In a small saucepan, heat the heavy cream over medium heat until it just begins to simmer. Pour the hot cream over the chopped chocolate and let it sit for 1-2 minutes.
12. Stir the chocolate and cream together until smooth and glossy. Let the ganache cool slightly to thicken.
13. Once the ganache has thickened to a spreadable consistency, frost the cooled cupcakes using a spoon or spatula.
14. Optionally, garnish the frosted cupcakes with fresh blueberries.
15. Serve and enjoy these Chocolate Blueberry Cupcakes as a delightful treat!

These Chocolate Blueberry Cupcakes combine the rich flavor of chocolate with the sweetness of fresh blueberries for a delicious and indulgent dessert. They're perfect for parties, gatherings, or as a special treat for yourself!

www.ingramcontent.com/pod-product-compliance
Lightning Source LLC
LaVergne TN
LVHW081610060526
838201LV00054B/2175